# playing
# with plays

## by Nicholas Barter

plays by Richard Blythe
photography by Nick Birch

unicorn

Macdonald Educational.
This book is produced with the help of
Unicorn Theatre children's workshops

# Contents

Have you ever been bored on a rainy day and felt you'd like to put on a play with your friends? Have you wanted to celebrate a birthday party by entertaining the guests? Or at school have you learned about a period of history and felt you'd like to perform a play to show how you imagine it might have been.

But you don't know where to begin. It seems rather a difficult thing to do. You feel you need a little help.

That is what this book is all about. It is a book full of games and ideas to help you experiment with your own imagination. Every time you play a 'let's pretend' game with your friends, you are really making up a little play. This book shows you how you can very easily change those games into play-making, perhaps for an audience to watch, if you feel that adventurous.

All you need is yourself and your friends, your imagination, and a little space to play in. You don't need any special equipment or any special skills.

Anyone can do it. You just have to want to.

First published 1979
Macdonald Educational Ltd
Holywell House, Worship Street
London EC2

© Macdonald Educational Ltd 1979

ISBN 0 356 06544 8

# Movement, mime, signals and signs

The first thing you have to do when you play with someone new is to get to know them.

This is how we're going to start our book. In this chapter you will find some enjoyable games which will help you to work well with your friends.

First find a space in the room, not too close to anyone else, or to the walls. Now stretch as far as you can. Stretch high; stretch wide. As though you have woken after a long sleep. Stretch to the tips of your fingers and the tips of your toes. Give a huge yawn to stretch your face. Without moving your feet, see how far you can reach all around you.

**Warming up exercises.**
*Explore the space in all directions with your hands. Mark out how much of the space around you is yours. Choose a partner. Stretch out your arms and rest your hands on each other's shoulders, then drop your arms to your sides. Imagine that one of your feet is nailed to the floor. It can't be moved at all. But you can move the other foot as much as you like. Practise.*

*The aim of the game is to touch each other in the middle of the back without letting your partner touch you. You musn't try to catch and hold each other's hands. Just move your body and your one free foot.*

Next you need to practise working very closely with your partner. Here is a mirror game to help you do this.

Face each other again, with your hands on each other's shoulders. Then drop your arms to your sides. Decide which of you is going to be leader in the game, and which is going to follow. You can change over the next time you play the game.

The leader makes a slow movement – like raising an arm, or a leg, or putting his or her head on one side. The partner must follow the movement exactly, as though they are a reflection in the mirror.

If you look into each other's eyes you will find the game easier to play. If you are the leader, don't try to trick your partner, but help them to play the game well by making movements which are easy to follow. After a while you can try ordinary things like brushing your teeth or combing your hair or doing up shirt buttons. You'll find it is more difficult than you think!

5

When you play games with your friends, you often
pretend to be different people and do different things.
Making a play is just the same. It is really only people
pretending to do something together.

If you want to pretend to be like someone else, you
need to be able to watch other people very carefully and
notice how they move and talk. Here's a game to get
you used to observing other people.

Choose a new partner and sit facing them. Look
closely at each other – at clothes, shoes, hair –
everything you can. Then turn your backs on each other
and change three things about your appearance. Roll
up a sleeve or untie a shoe lace or take off a bracelet. It
must be something your partner can see, not something
hidden. Then face each other again, and see if each of
you can guess what the other has changed.

When you are out walking, watch how people do their
work. Watch people washing their cars, or digging the
ground before they plant vegetables. Watch workers on
a building site. Watch road menders. Watch people
sewing, cooking or cleaning. If you took away the car,
the spade, or the crane, the needle and thread, the
cooking pan or the broom, could you still recognise what
those people are doing?

Here is a game for guessing what people are doing. Sit in a circle. One person thinks of a job of work which involves movement. They get up and pretend to do that job. Think about the tools you would use. How big are they? How heavy? Do you have to use a lot of effort to do the job? Act it out very clearly so that other people can recognise what job it is. As soon as someone else guesses, they must get up and join in. Don't talk. Don't copy the first person, but just try to help them, without using words. As each person guesses what the job is, they too must get up and join in, until you're all working away together.

For example, the first person might be washing a car with a bucket and cloth. The next person might bring the water hose to rinse the car, the third turn on the tap which lets the water into the hose, the fourth get a dry cloth to wipe the car, the fifth fetch a tin of wax, and the sixth polish the windscreen.

Once you have become good at playing this game, you can go right ahead and make a play out of it. Any one of you can think of something to do. Perhaps you're walking along the street, you slip on a banana skin and break your leg. Somebody comes to help you. Someone phones for an ambulance. The ambulance arrives and takes you to hospital. The doctor decides to operate.

You can see how one action can lead to another, and a very simple action at the beginning – falling down and showing that you've hurt yourself – can start you on quite a complicated story which you can all tell without using a single word.

Another way to start the game is for one of you to call out an idea – like 'factory' or 'bank robbery' or 'birthday party'. Someone else starts an action, and the others join in. Before you know it, you've made a play.

Here's another game. Choose a partner. One of you is going to be the sculptor, and the other the statue. You can change over the next time you play it. The sculptor bends the statue's arms and legs into different positions. Take care that you do this carefully so that you do not hurt your partner. Every time you move your partner, you make a new statue. Make the statue look like someone fighting, or someone washing the dishes, or someone climbing the stairs, or anything else you can think of. Then you and another sculptor can put your statues together so that they tell a story.

Add more statues, until all the statues in the group are telling a story – like a photograph taken just after a goal has been scored, or after a car has knocked someone over in the street.

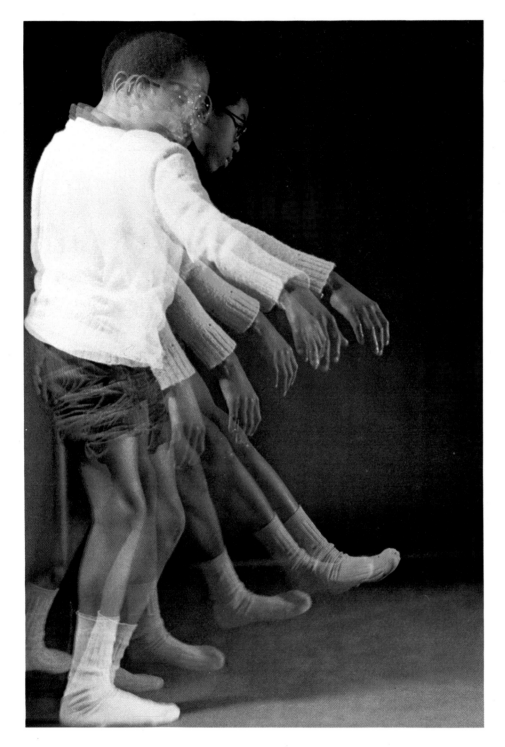

*Tell a story in slow motion, like an action replay on television or a slow motion film. For example, you could decide to play a sport – kick a football or throw a ball.*

It is also fun to tell a story in slow motion – like an action replay on television. You could run a race, but run it as though you are up to your waist in something sticky and gluey, like treacle. Show how difficult it is to move your legs, how hard you have to pull to get them out of the treacle. Or play a tennis match in slow motion, holding an imaginary racket. Show, by the way you look at the invisible ball, exactly where it is. Watch it come over the net to you. Watch it bounce high so that you have to leap to reach it. Run from one side of the court to the other and hit it with a good strong swing of the make-believe racket.

Tennis is a sport which some of you can watch as though you are a crowd. For example, if you are watching the slow motion tennis match, see if you can follow the flight of the ball over the net. All your heads should turn from side to side at the same time. Make your eyes follow the players when they look at the ball.

Acting without speaking, as we have been doing in all these games, is called 'mime'. When you mime a story you must make it clear by your actions exactly where you are and what you are doing. You have no words to help you. On the next page is a mime game to help you do this really well.

Pretend that you are trapped somewhere – in a prison cell, or a lift, or a cage. Now mime how you escape in such a way that your friends watching can guess exactly where you are escaping from. Think about the place you are trapped in. Are there walls? How far from you are they? Put your hands flat on them. Are there bars? Can you get your fingers round them? Are there doors or windows? How big? Closed or open? How difficult is it to escape?

Then show how you do escape. Perhaps you find a key on the floor. Or you climb on a chair to squeeze through a window. Or perhaps you are very strong and can bend the bars of your cage or prison cell and squeeze your body slowly through.

Here is another mime game. Two of you decide on an object which is so big that it takes two of you to carry it. Then see if you can carry it in such a way that your friends watching can discover what the invisible object is. Imagine your object in detail. How big is it? How heavy? Is it slippery and difficult to hold on to? Or perhaps it has things that stick out and make it difficult to reach round it. Perhaps it is very long. Get clear in your imagination exactly what kind of shape it is.

All this time we have been using imaginary objects to tell our stories. It can be just as much fun to use real objects, but pretend they are quite different things.

*See if you can carry the invisible object in such a way that your friends watching can discover what it is.*

*When miming you should think hard about the shape objects make. If you pick up something imaginary, show the space it makes in your hands. Keep your hands in that shape all the time you are carrying it.*

*When you mime lifting or putting something down, do it so that people can see how heavy or light the object is, or whether it is easily broken.*

*When you mime a story you have no words to help you.*

*You have to show how you peeled an orange . . .*

*. . . then broke it in half.*

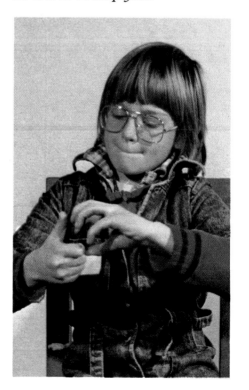

*At first it tasted good . . .*

*. . . but then you began to think it wasn't so tasty after all!*

*. . . and after a while you began to feel really rather ill . . .*

Objects used in play-making are called 'properties' or 'props' for short. Here is a game to play with props in which the prop itself makes up the story. All you need is an object like a broom or a bucket or a hair brush – something very ordinary and familiar.

Sit in a circle. Pass the prop around the circle for each of you to have a close look at it. You will soon realise that it doesn't just look like a hair brush or a broom. You can imagine it being many other things. The brush could be a pop singer's microphone, or a gun or a telephone. The broom could be a canoe paddle or a vacuum cleaner, a guitar or other musical instrument.

Whatever the idea that comes into your head, act using the prop as the new object you imagine it to be. Your friends have to guess what the new object is. Then pass the prop on to the next person. Each person in the circle should try to think of a different use for it.

Once you've played the game this way, change it. Collect a number of different props. Start the game again by one person acting something, using one prop. As soon as someone else guesses what they're doing they should get up and join in. They must not copy, but should add to the first person's activity, using their own prop as something different.

*You will soon see that it doesn't just look like a broom. It could be a gun, a guitar or a trumpet, weights, a horse . . .*

The more each of you believes that your own prop is what you want it to be – the more your friends will also imagine it as you see it. In fact you could play any of the mime games we've already talked about, using a prop. For example, one person could use the prop to start a story without words. Then they could pass the prop and the story on round the circle. Each person then has to add to the story, pretending the prop is the same object as in the first person's part of the story, but taking the story on a little bit further each time.

Here are some more prop games. Take a ball and throw or pass it to each other, keeping moving all the time. One person decides that the ball is now made of iron. You must throw it to each other as though it is terribly, terribly heavy. Then someone cries 'we are old'. So now you all behave like a lot of old people trying to throw or roll this heavy iron ball to each other. Someone else can shout 'it's light again', but remember that you are still old until someone says 'we're young'. Or perhaps 'we are babies', and you have to pass the ball like babies crawling about the floor. Also try passing the ball as though it is very hot, or very cold. Or very slippery, or furry. Or very soft and cushiony. Think of other ways the ball could feel, and try them.

# Plays without words

Here are a few stories for you to mime. Some have endings, but some have not because it is up to you to invent them. These stories can all be quite different each time they are acted.

One of the most interesting ways to play with these plays is to get two or three groups of people to do the same mime, then you can compare them.

### Blown down

Some people on a camping holiday are busy unpacking and putting their tent up. There is a strong wind, and as they work, the wind starts to blow more strongly, making their task more and more difficult. What happens?

Some people are standing in groups, chatting and drinking tea in one of those big tents they sometimes have at summer fêtes. They listen as the wind rises, and joke about what might happen if the wind becomes so strong that it blows the tent down. The wind does get stronger, and stronger. Now continue the story.

### A surprise

The Wizard Merlin leads the bravest knights and fairest ladies of Britain to where a jewelled sword is stuck in a huge stone or rock. He explains to them that the knight who can pull the sword out of the stone will become king and make his country great. Several knights try. But the sword is stuck fast. No one can move it. Then, to everyone's surprise, Merlin points to the boy called Arthur. Arthur does not want to try, but Merlin and one or two others say he should. Arthur goes to the stone and easily draws out the sword. He looks at it in astonishment, then hands it to Merlin. Merlin kneels and offers the sword for Arthur to take again. Arthur does so and, as he takes it, he realises, and so do all the others, that he is now king and the new leader of Britain.

### Held up

A lot of people run into a station to catch a train that is just about to leave. At the gate where passengers show their tickets to the ticket-collector, one of them has to search through all his or her pockets, but cannot find the ticket. This holds everybody else up. They think they are going to miss their train.

What happens next?

### King of the golden touch

Midas was king of the ancient land of Phrygia. One day he was with his daughter and courtiers when he was visited by a god.

The god tells the king that he may have one wish, and it will come true. Midas greedily wishes that everything he touches shall turn to gold. The god grants the wish, and disappears. Midas notices that the clothes he is wearing have already turned to gold. So has his chair. He is delighted, and everyone is amazed. Someone brings him food and drink. The goblet turns to gold as soon as he touches it. But so does the food he tries to eat. Everyone looks puzzled. Midas's daughter goes to her father to see what has happened. The king touches her, and she becomes a golden statue. The king turns to his courtiers for help, but everyone moves away in horror.

### No smoking

Some of you are on a train, in a 'no smoking' carriage. A man gets in. He lights a big, smelly pipe and starts to read his newspaper. You all hope one of the others will ask him to stop smoking.

But no one does. So in the end one or two of you try in other ways to make the man realise he is doing something that you do not like. What do you do?

### Shipwrecked

Some people have been stranded on a desert island. One of them sees a ship in the far distance, and tells the others. A few of them start waving, but the ship is too far away for anyone on it to see. They try other ways of attracting the ship's attention, and in the end they are successful. (What did they do to attract the ship's attention?) The ship turns towards them. But they have also attracted the attention of someone else on the island. Who is it? Continue the story yourselves.

### Locked out

You are carrying a big parcel of precious glass. It needs both arms to hold it. It is pouring with rain as you leave your house with the parcel. You shut the front door behind you, and it locks. But you cannot move. Your coat is caught in the door.

You knock for someone inside to open the door and free you. But no one comes. You are trying to release yourself when a big dog comes along the road and starts snarling and snapping at your legs. What do you do?

You can end the story there, or another person can join in. This person is walking along and goes to the rescue when he or she hears a dog barking and someone calling for help. What happens next?

Or you can change the story by changing the people in it. Who is this second person? A policeman? The owner of the dog? Is it a thief who wants to steal the parcel? Just a passer-by?

Or you can change the story in a different way, using props. Give the first person a real parcel to hold. Give the second person another parcel.

What do you think could be in the second parcel? Meat, which the dog smells? Or is it big and, like the other parcel, almost impossible to hold with only one arm? Or is it full of something that is easily broken? How do you both work the problem out? What if a crowd of people stop and watch or try to help? See if you can continue the story from here.

### A public performance

Two people are arranging a display in a shop-window. They start fooling about, first to amuse themselves and then to amuse the passers-by in the street. A small crowd collects to watch the fun. They encourage the people in the window to do sillier and sillier things.

Then the owner of the shop comes along the street. He is pleased to see so many people looking in his shop-window. He joins them, to see what has attracted their attention. Then he realises what is happening.

Now you continue the story yourselves.

## Won't they be surprised!

You have been to a pet shop to buy an animal. Now you bring it home in the basket or box which the shop gave to you. You put the container on the floor to show your family the surprise you have for them. They gather round. You lift the lid. The man in the pet shop has given you the wrong basket. There is something nasty inside! What is it? What happens next?

## King and queen for a day

As a reward for faithful service, a king and a queen let two of their servants rule for a day. Everyone thinks this is a huge joke. Gleefully the servant king and queen try out their new power. They can make laws that will last for just one day. They can do and say just what they want. They can wear beautiful clothes and fe.st on food and drink. They will be entertained and waited on hand and foot by their fellow servants and even by the real king and queen.

But then they start enjoying themselves in most extravagant and unexpected ways. Will the real king and queen still enjoy the joke, and will the courtiers, too?

The clock strikes midnight. The servants' special day is over. They no longer have the power of a king and queen.

Now what happens?

## The great meeting

Columbus sailed from Europe across the Atlantic nearly five hundred years ago and discovered a continent which he had not known was there – the land of America. To him and his sailors it must have been just like going to another planet. In fact, they called this place 'the New World'. They did not know what to expect. Perhaps monsters. Perhaps people with mysterious, magical powers. Or dangerous people. Columbus's men just did not know what they might find.

Imagine you are Columbus's sailors. You have been at sea for many, many weeks without seeing land. The ocean seemed so enormous that you thought you might never reach land again, but might sail on and on until you died, all alone on the empty, endless sea.

Now you have sighted land. You have just rowed ashore from your ship to visit it. You pull your boat up on the beach and look around you. Is the sand really sand, like at home? What are those trees and plants over there? You have never seen anything like them before. You see and hear strange birds. Suddenly, one of you thinks something moved in the trees. One of the Indians who live in this land appears. You are just as strange to him as he is to you. He has never seen people with white faces, or people dressed as you are.

Other Indians from a nearby village slowly appear. The two groups look at each other, wondering among themselves. Then someone from one of the groups advances. Then another. Very slowly the two groups move closer. Everyone is frightened and curious, all at the same time. Then they meet.

Think hard about this, until you really feel what it must have been like to be one of those Indians or one of those sailors. If you think hard you will have a good idea of what that meeting must have been like, nearly five hundred years ago.

# Words, games, stories and tales

The next step in making our plays is to learn some games which help us to discover how the people or 'characters' in our stories could talk to each other. When characters talk in a play, the words they speak are called 'dialogue' which comes from two Greek words meaning 'two speaking'. When the dialogue is made up as we go along, rather than thought out and written down beforehand, we say that the actors are 'improvising' the dialogue. The games in this chapter are all about how to improvise your own dialogue. When you play them, listen carefully to what each of you has to say. Listening is as important as speaking!

*When you play word games, listen carefully to each other. Listening is just as important as speaking! And when it is your turn to speak, speak clearly so that everyone can hear.*

*Keep your clapping rhythm going steadily, whatever happens.*

*Don't try to trick each other. Think of yourselves as partners or teams, all trying to help each other play the games as well as you can.*

It is important not to try to trick each other. Think of yourselves as partners or teams, all trying to help each other play the different games as well as you can. Don't all try to talk at the same time. When it isn't your turn, watch your friends quietly and with interest, and listen to what they say in the game.

First of all, here are some games to help you think up words very quickly. Start by sitting in a circle on the floor. You'll need a ball or a shoe – anything which can be passed easily from hand to hand. Someone sits in the middle of the circle, holding the 'ball'; next they shout out a letter of the alphabet, at the same time throwing the 'ball' to someone in the circle. The person who catches it at once passes it round the circle and says as many words beginning with that letter as they can. When the ball gets back to them, they can go into the centre, throw the ball to someone new, giving them a different letter of the alphabet.

When you play this game, the person who calls out the letter and the person who has to think up the words should think of each other as partners, trying to beat the others in the circle. Don't give your partner a difficult letter, but try to give them one which begins lots of words.

Here is another word game. You have to listen very carefully and speak very clearly. The rest of the group must be able to hear you.

Form a circle and sit on the floor. First learn a simple clapping rhythm: two claps with your hands together and then one quiet one with your hands on your knees. Not too fast. CLAP-CLAP-pat, CLAP-CLAP-pat, CLAP-CLAP-pat. In the game you can only speak on the 'soft beat', when everyone is patting their knees.

First, one person says a word – any word they can think of. The person sitting on their left waits for the soft beat to come round, then says a word which is in some way to do with the first. For example, the first word might be 'pen'. The next person could say 'ink' and the next one 'bottle'; the next 'milk', the next 'cow' and the next 'grass'. Each word is suggested only by the one immediately before it, but you end up with a quite different word from the one you started with.

If you get really stuck and can't think of a word
which is to do with the last one, choose a word which
rhymes instead; after 'pen' you could say 'hen' or 'den'

Each person in the group has three lives. If you miss
the 'soft beat', and don't say a word, you lose a life.

After you've lost three lives, you have to drop out of
the game. The game goes on until the last two people
compete to be winner. If you become really good at this
game, try playing it with two words going the opposite
way round the circle. It is really quite difficult, so don't
get upset if you can't do it well! All sorts of new things
can happen when you use the words to make up a play.

*When the storyteller introduces a character to the story, someone 'volunteers' to be that character, and mimes the activities which the storyteller describes. Use props if you want to. Turn them into different things as you find that you need them.*

You could put all the words from the last game together, and see what sort of story you can make.

Sit in a circle. Go round the circle once playing your word game: for example, it could go something like this: clap clap 'ship', clap clap 'sail', clap clap 'mast'. Each person must remember the word they said.

Now go back to the beginning. Each person now has to say a sentence using their word. The first person could begin the story with something like, 'Once upon a time I was sailing along in my brand new ship.'

As each person uses up their word, they pass the story on to the next person in the circle, who has to add to it. So the next person might say '. . . it was a beautiful day, and the wind filled the sail . . .' and the next person could continue '. . . suddenly, there was a terrible crack and the mast broke.'

Here is another way to make up stories. Someone says the first word of the story, such as 'once'; the next person says 'upon', and the next 'a' and the next 'time'; and the next says 'there', the next says 'lived', and so it goes on. By each of you thinking up a single word, you have very soon made up a story that none of you would have imagined.

Now that we've invented our stories, it's time to act them out as well. In some of the mime games we tried to make our actions very interesting and very clear. In the same way, we have to make the actions in our story here very clear. Here is a good game for acting out a story using all you've learnt about mime. The game is called 'volunteers'.

Choose two people from the group to be storytellers. They start to tell the story in just the same way as in the game we've just played. They pass the story to each other to continue. But now, when they introduce a character, someone from the circle jumps up and 'volunteers' to be that character. Don't talk about it. Just mime the story which the two storytellers are telling. It is important that the storytellers speak clearly so that the 'volunteer' actors know exactly what they are supposed to do. Use props if you want to. Turn them into different things as you need them. Each of you can have a turn at being the storyteller and an actor.

Now it's time to invent some dialogue for your characters. We're going to play 'speaking volunteers'. This time the storytellers also narrate what the characters say to each other. Keep the sentences quite short so the actors can remember them easily. For example the storyteller might say, 'And the wizard said, "Leave my house or I will turn you into a frog."'

*Using objects in your games can lead you into some interesting stories. Each person can start a story about the object, then pass the story on round the circle, for other people to add to it.*

The volunteer actors must repeat the exact words given to them by the storyteller, so they have to listen very carefully.

In 'speaking volunteers' the storytellers have made up the plot and the dialogue. But you can play the game so that the storytellers and the characters add to the story together. Choose two new storytellers who start a story just as in 'volunteers'. But this time they do not say what the character would say. They stop at, 'and the wizard said'. Now it is the actors' turn to make up what the character says, and the storytellers who have to listen very carefully. The actor may say something they don't expect! They will have to take up the story and continue it, so that it all fits together and makes sense.

Don't try to make the story too difficult. Storytellers and actors should all work together as a team. Storytellers must leave time in the story for the actors to act out the story. Volunteer actors must act the story that is being told as closely as possible.

When you played the prop game you turned one object into many different things. Each one of these could have been the beginning of a different story.

Collect six objects – quite simple things like a bucket or broom or piece of chalk or just a tin can.

*Try to make the object as important in your part of the story as possible.*

*You can also play games where each of you uses the object as a different thing in your part of the story.*

Sit in a circle with one person in the middle. The person in the middle picks up an object and hands it to someone in the circle, who has to start telling a story about that object. The story is then passed on round the circle, for other people to add to it. Give different objects to different people.

Give out all six objects at once to different people. Start the story at one point and pass it round the circle. Each person has to bring their object into the story just as you had to bring your word into the connecting word game. You must try to make the object as important in your part of the story as possible. But also try to make sure you are all telling bits of the same story.

If you want to concentrate on making your dialogue as interesting as possible, there are some enjoyable telephone games to help you. When playing telephone games you have to make believe that there is really someone at the other end of the telephone line; you have to leave enough space in your conversation for the imaginary person to say things. You must pretend to be listening to them and reply. Use any object you like as the telephone, or just pretend you have one. Choose a partner. One of you pretends the phone is ringing, picks it up, listens, then hands it to the other.

At the same time, give them a piece of information or a clue about the phone call. You could say 'I'm afraid it is bad news', or 'It's your father, he sounds very excited', or anything else you think of. Your partner must continue the phone call, making a full story out of the single clue you have given them. Remember that no one else can hear the imaginary person at the other end of the telephone. So you have to make clear exactly what has happened by what you say. Leave enough time between your words for the imaginary caller to speak. Try to end the story by saying something interesting to finish it off.

Now try playing a different game altogether. One of you picks up the telephone and pretends to telephone for something you need. For example you could ask someone to come and repair the television so that you can watch your favourite programme. Or you could complain about the noise your neighbours are making and ask them to be quiet. Or ring up and ask about a job you have seen advertised. Again, you have to continue the dialogue with the imaginary person, by replying to what you imagine they are saying.

When you can do this well, you can add another bit to the game. While you are having the phone conversation, try to tell your partner what the person on the other end is saying. You have to continue to talk on the phone and in between tell your partner what the person on the phone has said to you. It's quite difficult, but it is great fun. After a while your partner can advise you on how you should reply!

Have you noticed how when people talk to each other, they often give clues about the kind of work they do?

Choose a partner. One of you walk up to the other and ask a question which tells them what kind of work they do. For example, you could ask, 'May I have a ticket to Birmingham please?' or 'Is my car ready yet?' Without having said 'you are a railway ticket seller' or 'you are a garage-man,' you have still told your partner what their job is. Your partner should try to carry on the conversation.

Here is a different question game. Ask your partner a question which tells them something else about themselves. 'Do you always bump your head on the top of the door when you walk into a room?' Or 'it must be difficult not being able to see over the heads of the crowd.' The first question could say that your partner is very tall, or both very tall and very clumsy! The second question could mean your partner is very small, or that they've hurt themselves and are in a wheel chair.

*Storytellers and actors should work together as a team, storytellers leaving enough time in the story for the actors to act, and the actors listening carefully to the story. If you work together like this, you will find that your ideas can become more and more exciting. All kinds of interesting and unexpected things can happen when both storytellers and actors are adding to the story together.*

These games show you how you can invent characters in the course of your play simply by asking questions of each other. It is just like the game we played in which you made your partner into a statue by putting their arms and legs in different positions. Only this time you're making your character by the words you use in speaking to them.

Have you noticed that when people talk to each other, sometimes one person has more to say, or leads the conversation, or seems to know best, and bosses the other people around? Sometimes the people they're talking to are quite happy with this.

But sometimes they are not happy with it at all. Then the conversation becomes a struggle of words, in which everyone tries to show they know better than others.

It can be very interesting to try out this kind of conversation in your dialogue games and find out how it goes on. Sometimes a real argument starts. At the same time you often find out, curiously, how some things can become very funny.

Here is a game called 'see-saws'. Get into groups of four. Two of you are going to be actors in the scene and the other two will stand next to the actors, one at each side. These people will stand up or crouch down, like people on a see-saw, when the actor they are next to is either getting the best of the struggle, or the worst.

Start the game by one asking the other a question, as in the game we have just played. The actors have to carry on the conversation, each trying to show that they know best. Meanwhile, the 'see-saw' people show how the conversation is going. When their actor seems to be getting the best of the conversation, or seems to know best, they stand up tall. When their actor is getting the worst, they crouch down low. Listen carefully.

Sometimes your character may say something which puts him or her back on top, and then you have to stand up. Next thing you know you will have to crouch down once again!

Now try the game a bit differently, so that one of the characters tries to make the other feel good by telling them that they know best. Character A asks the question, but does it to make Character B feel that Character B knows best. If you play the game this way, you'll find it will have a very happy feeling.

All the time the see-saw people should show how the conversation is going.

Then try it with *both* characters making the other one feel that he or she knows best. When you play it this way, the see-saw people had better start by sitting on the floor! By the end you could find you are both stretching in order to stand up the taller. Surprisingly, if you listen to this version of the game, it is often very funny to hear people go on trying to make each other feel important for so long.

Two people both trying to give the feeling that they themselves know best makes a struggle of words and perhaps an angry scene. On the other hand, if one person seems to know best and the other one agrees, then there's no struggle or argument, and that makes a calm scene.

You can use these ideas when you're making up a play later on. If you need an argument to take place, or need a friendly or calm scene to happen, you can play this game to find out how.

So far we have talked about actions with no words, and stories with both words and actions. What about storytelling where you have no actions to help you and you have to tell the story using only sounds?

It can be quite fun to find out how some of the stories you have invented would sound if you had no actions to help you with the story, only sounds – just as if it was a radio play. You can't see people going out of a room, only hear the noises – opening and shutting doors, walking across the floor. You can't see them acting pouring out tea – only hear the sounds of clinking cups and gurgling liquid.

Here are some games which help you to imagine how your play would have to be if you only had words and sounds with which to tell it.

For the first game you need some props. Work in pairs, one of you closing your eyes and the other using the prop to make a sound. You could be sweeping the floor, or pouring a drink, or turning the pages of a book.

*The see-saw people show how the conversation is going. When their actor seems to know best, they stand up tall. When their actor is getting the worst of the conversation, they crouch down low.*

*The partner, with eyes closed, has to guess which actions can be understood and which are impossible to understand by just listening.*

The partner, with eyes still closed, has to guess which actions can be understood and which are impossible to understand by just listening. Experiment with many different actions – walking, sitting down, moving furniture about.

In this way you can discover the activities which you must describe in your dialogue, and others which are clear just by listening to them.

Another game goes like this. Work in groups of four. Two of you shut your eyes. The other two decide on an activity for both of you to do together. For example, one of you could wash up the dishes and the other dry them, or both of you could cut down a tree.

You can give each other instructions and talk about what you are doing, but you must not name the job. You can't say 'It is hard cutting down the tree', but you could say 'this saw is rather blunt and the wood is a bit hard'. The other pair have to guess what you are doing.

*Experiment with many different actions – walking, sitting down, moving furniture, using plates and cups . . .*

If you really want to make your play into a 'radio' play, you could use a tape recorder to record it. To do it really well, you should work out your story and your dialogue, decide on your sound effects, and then write it all down, so that you can all read the words, and know exactly when you should say things, or make sounds.

Using a tape recorder can be a great help in getting your play as you want it. You could tape record yourself playing some of the storytelling games in this chapter. Then listen to the tape recorder and pick out the bits that you think work really well. If you want to, you could write them down. Then you could play the game again, and tape more good bits. Or simply play the games and write down the bits you liked, without using the tape recorder. Then think about the characters and the story. What other things can you imagine the characters saying? Write them down and see if they work. Then play the game again.

# Plays to act to storytelling

In the first play here, only two people speak. They are the storytellers, who read the story aloud. Each time these speakers pause, the actors mime what has just been said. If there are not enough of you to play all the parts, you can each play more than one. Divide these parts among you: two speakers, two ladies, two men, people in the crowd, some town-councillors, the mayor, the Pied Piper, and the children of the town.

### The Pied Piper's revenge

**Speaker 1**  One day, in the town of Hamelin, there was a meeting in the market square. The mayor and his councillors stood on a high platform, and the people of the town gathered round them. The people were very angry. The mayor was trying to make a speech, and the councillors were waving for silence.

**Speaker 2**  'Quiet! Quiet!' called the councillors.

**Speaker 1**  'This town is over-run with rats!' shouted one lady. 'Just look at them – running about everywhere!'

**Speaker 2**  'Shoo, rats, shoo!' cried another lady. 'Get away!'

**Speaker 1**  'There!' said the first lady. 'One of them has just bitten my foot! Get away! Get away!'

**Speaker 2**  'Just look at my best Sunday hat!' cried one man loudly. 'The rats made a nest in it!'

**Speaker 1**  'Those rats frighten me!' sobbed the first lady, and she nearly fainted.

**Speaker 2**  'Never mind, my dear,' said a man to her, comfortingly. 'There, there – don't cry.'

**Speaker 1**  The rats were scampering everywhere, and the loud-voiced man got very angry, shouting, 'You town-councillors must clear this town of rats!'

    Everybody in the crowd agreed. They shoo-ed at the rats and told one another what a silly man the mayor was. And as for the town-councillors – well! But the mayor and the councillors could think of nothing. They whispered and scratched their heads, and looked very serious and sad. And all the time the people had to keep jumping away from the rats.

**Speaker 2**  Then, very mysteriously, a stranger appeared. Everyone looked, and fell silent. The stranger was a tall man, all dressed in red and yellow. He carried a little pipe, like a flute, on a ribbon round his neck. A tall councillor was the first to speak. 'Go away!' he said. But the mayor twiddled his thumbs and thought. 'Can you do anything about these rats?' he asked at last.

**Speaker 1**  And the stranger said, 'Yes, I can clear your town of rats. I am called the Pied Piper. If you will give me a thousand gilders I will clear the rats with this.' And he blew a tune on his pipe.

**Speaker 2**  'How can he do it with that?' wondered the crowd.

**Speaker 1**  'Ho-hum,' thought the mayor. And then he said, 'All right. We'll give you a thousand gilders.'

**Speaker 2**  The Piper bowed and smiled. And then he started to play, and as he did so he marched round and round.

30

**Speaker 1**  'Look!' cried the councillors. 'The rats are following him!' Everyone watched and wondered.

'Bless my soul!' said the mayor. 'Just look – they're coming out of the houses, too!' And he shook hands with the councillors, and the people cheered.

Away marched the Pied Piper, blowing on his pipe. And all the rats followed him.

**Speaker 2**  The people watched. Then they hugged each other, and they slapped each other on the back for joy.

**Speaker 1**  'Just look!' cried a councillor, pointing from where he stood, high up on the platform. 'He's taking the rats to the river!'

**Speaker 2**  And another councillor jumped for joy. 'He's drowning them!' he told the people. 'The rats are all tumbling into the river!'

**Speaker 1**  At that, all the people rushed off after the Piper, eager to see the end of the rats.

**Speaker 2**  But the mayor and his councillors stayed behind and whispered secretly to each other. They behaved very strangely, and started to look very pleased.

**Speaker 1**  Soon, the Pied Piper came back. 'There you are,' he said. 'I've done it. So please pay me my thousand gilders.'

**Speaker 2**  The mayor and the councillors smiled at each other. 'Oh, no,' said the mayor. 'Those rats are dead. We saw them drown. They can't come back now, whether we pay you or not. So we won't.'

**Speaker 1**  At this, the Piper was filled with terrible rage. 'I shall make you sorry for this!' he shouted. And he started to play his pipe.

**Speaker 2**  In ones and twos the children began to appear.

**Speaker 1**  They listened to the Piper's playing, and some of them started to dance.

**Speaker 2**  And then the Piper began marching round and round. The mayor frowned, and the councillors looked frightened. And the children followed the Piper, dancing, as he played his pipe.

**Speaker 1**  And then he marched away, still playing. And all the children danced away with him.

**Speaker 2**  The mayor and councillors stared after them in horror. And then at each other in a terrible fear.

**Speaker 1**  The people of the town returned from the river – the mothers and fathers, the aunts and uncles, the grandmothers and grandfathers, the godmothers and godfathers.

**Speaker 2**  'What is that music we can hear?' they asked.

**Speaker 1**  And when the mayor tried to explain, and when the councillors pointed to where the Piper and the children had gone. . .

**Speaker 2**  Some of the people started throwing things. . .

**Speaker 1**  And some of them rushed after the children. And then the rest joined them. . .

**Speaker 2**  Until only the mayor and the councillors were left, holding their heads or crying into their handkerchiefs. And all for the sake of that thousand gilders!

31

In this next play there is only one storyteller and the actors speak their parts, by repeating the words the storyteller gives them each time he or she pauses. The characters are: a storyteller, the king, the queen, the nurse, some courtiers and soldiers, six good fairies, and one bad fairy.

## The seven gifts

Many, many years ago, there was a king who ruled over an enchanted kingdom. Everything there was magical and wonderful and happy. But not the king. He was sad. He often wondered why, and one day, as he sat alone, the answer came to him. 'I know!' he said. 'It's because the queen and I have no children.'

Just then a nurse came hurrying in. 'Your majesty,' she said, 'I have wonderful news!'

And the king said, 'Ah, Nurse, but will it make me happy?' The nurse told him it would. 'Oh, yes,' she said. 'The queen has just had a lovely new baby girl!'

Straightaway the king and the nurse did a little dance for joy. Then the king said, 'Nurse, please ask the queen to bring the baby to me.' The nurse bustled away, all breathless and flustered and excited. The king went back to his throne, where he bounced up and down with happiness.

Back came the nurse with the queen, who was carrying the baby and crying, 'Look, husband, look!' And the king looked at the baby, and the queen looked, and the nurse looked. And they all sighed together, one big, long drawn-out 'Ah!'

Suddenly, the king said, 'We must have a party!' And the queen said, 'What a lovely idea! Who shall we ask?'

The king thought for a moment, and then replied, 'We must ask the good fairies.' The queen clapped her hands, and the king did another little dance with *her*. Then the nurse said, 'Your majesty, I have already asked the good fairies, all six of them.'

And then in came the courtiers, two by two. And two by two they bowed to the baby. And in marched the soldiers, two by two. And two by two they saluted the baby. And then – in came the six good fairies, and they all carried presents for the baby. 'Health and happiness to your majesties!' they said.

The king and queen bowed their heads politely. 'Thank you, Good Fairies,' they answered. One by one, the fairies presented their gifts to the new princess.

Said the first: 'I bring this child the gift of knowledge.'
Said the second: 'I bring this child the gift of a loving heart.'
Said the third: 'I bring this child the gift of riches and wealth.'
Said the fourth: 'I bring this child the gift of gentle speech.'
Said the fifth: 'I bring this child the gift of great beauty.'

But then there was a huge *bang!* outside the room, and a harsh voice was heard crying, 'Why was I not asked to this party?' And again, 'I am the bad fairy! Let me enter!'

Everyone was very upset to hear this! In fact, everyone said things like 'Dear me!' and 'Tut-tut' and 'It's the bad fairy!'

But in the end the king had to say, 'I'm afraid we shall have to let her in.' So in swept the bad fairy. And very wicked she looked.

'Have you brought a present?' asked the king, as pleasantly as he could. 'Ho, yes!' said the bad fairy, with a sort of snarl.

Now continue the story of the Sleeping Beauty in your own way. You can easily remind each other how the story goes on.

# Masks, costumes, powder and paint

If you look at people at school, on the bus or train, have you noticed how different they are from each other? Everybody looks quite unlike everyone else.

In the games you have been playing you have been pretending to be many different kinds of people. And sometimes you will want the people in your plays to look just as they feel. To help this, we use make-up. Actors make their faces look older, younger, angrier or sadder, by the way they show up the lines on their faces. Or they make their eyes bigger. Or give themselves grey hair. Or change the colour of their skins to make themselves look as though they come from different countries.

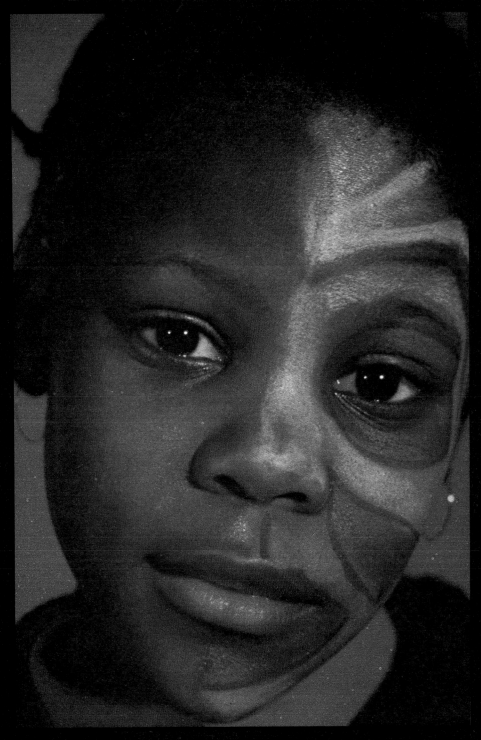

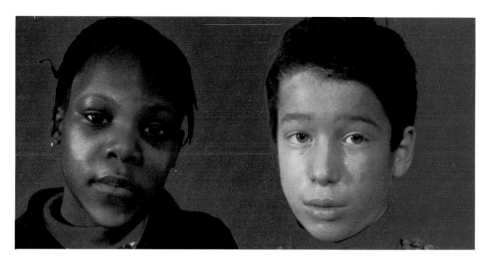

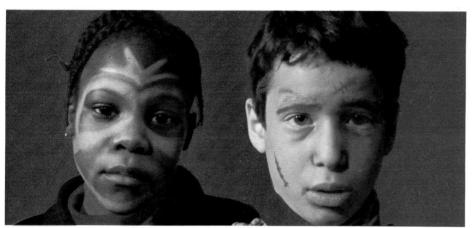

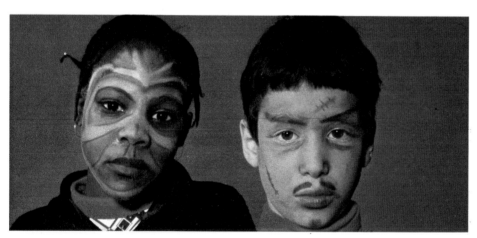

**An exotic make-up and one with scars.** *Spread a little cold cream on your face. It will make your skin easier to work on. Then wipe it off with a tissue. If you have black skin, you don't need to cover your face with a 'base', unless you want an exotic make-up with bright colour. Then use a white or cream-coloured base.*

*For white skin you need a light or cream base, or reddish brown if you want to look weather-beaten.*

*Flat areas like your forehead and cheeks are good places to put scars or to make patterns. But always try to follow the shape of your face. Don't crowd all the marks together on one part of your face, but spread them out.*

*To add scars to your face, draw the line very thinly with dark red or brown, and then show where the stitches went.*

*Now add the details. Put light colours beside dark ones on your exotic make-up. They show up better that way. Follow the line of the cheeks, but make a pattern of shadows. Use silver highlights. Make circles round your mouth and nose. Be bold.*

*Change your eyebrows. Cover your real eyebrows with skin-coloured base and draw in new ones with a dark pencil or face paint. Make them uneven and it looks strange and exciting. You can paint on beards and moustaches, too.*

Let's find out how you can make yourselves look different – like the character you want to play. At first it is interesting to find out how little you need to change. You can make yourself look quite different in all sorts of clever ways.

First of all, you can start with the shape of your face. You will need to be able to see yourself clearly, so you need quite a large mirror. Now look at your face very carefully. Sit facing a window, or arrange a lamp so that it shines on your face when you are looking into the mirror. Look hard at your face. You can see where the bumps and the dips are.

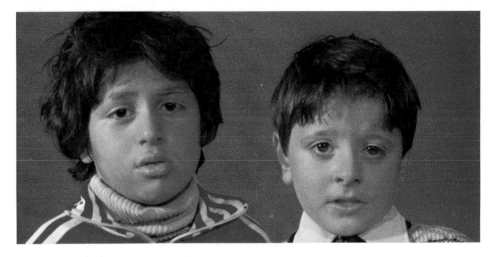

**Looking older or looking handsome.** *Make sure that the base is smooth and even, and goes all over your face. Right up to the line of your hair, under your chin, right up to your ears. Rub it well in. You can make your cheeks a little redder if you are healthy, make them pale if you are old and tired. Mix the colours to experiment. Everyone's skin is a slightly different shade.*

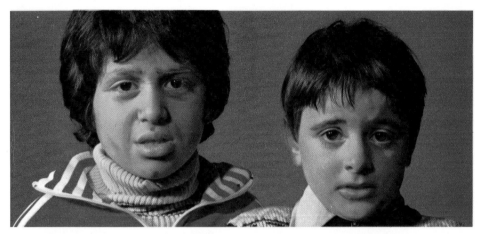

*Grey shadows make you look older. Screw up your face. See where the lines are. Look for the shadows. Use a make-up pencil or paint-brush to draw the lines very thin. Soften the shadows with the tip of your finger. Put the light colour along the bony bits that stick out.*

*Blue shadows above your eyes make you look handsome, grey shadows make you look old.*

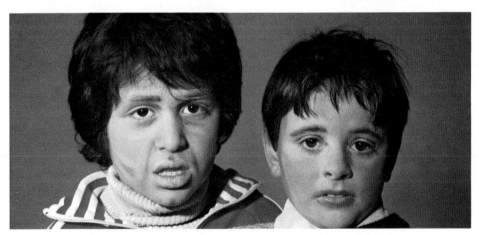

*Final details. Draw a thin line round your mouth with dark brown. Give yourself a cleft chin with a shadow in the centre of your chin. It looks deeper if you put light make-up each side of it. A red dot in the corner of your eye makes your eyes look brighter.*

*Finish your make-up by making sure everything is clear and neat. Then finally put face powder all over with cotton wool or a powder puff. This will hold the make-up together.*

Here's a good way to find out how light makes your face look different. Fetch a torch. Draw the curtains or turn off the light so that the room is dark. Face the mirror and hold the torch just below your chin, with the light shining up into your face. See how different you look. Now hold the torch over your head and shine the light down over your face. You look much older and sadder, don't you? There are shadows under your eyes. Your nose looks long and bony. Now hold the torch at the side of your face. Do you see how one side seems to stick out where the light catches it? The other side sinks back into the shadows.

When you make up, you are trying to get the effect that the torch gives. With make-up you make the deep, shadowy bits of your face deeper and more shadowy, so that they seem to sink in. You make the bony bits which stick out, stand out more clearly.

You really need only one or two colours of make-up to change your face quite a bit. Whatever colour skin you have, you need a make-up which is much lighter to use on the bits of your face which stick out. And if you have a white or very light skin, you need a make-up which is much darker than your skin (like the colour of the shadows when you shone the torch onto your face).

On this page there are some simple experiments with changing the shape of your face. As you try each one out, keep checking the effect by turning off the lamp and shining the torch on your face.

First, collect all the make-up you can. Ask your mother or her friends to let you have their old make-up. You can sometimes buy it quite cheaply at a chemist or large department store. To remove this kind of make-up, you spread cold cream all over your face and wipe it off with paper hankies. You may need to repeat this to get your face really clean. Then wash your face with soap and water. A little water and lots of soap will give you best results.

Washable face paints can also be great fun to use. You can buy them in many toy shops.

When you are ready to start making up your face, put on an old shirt to protect your clothes. Keep lots of paper hankies near you, so that you can wipe off mistakes and start again.

*Using highlights on your face. Take a light-coloured or white make-up or face paint and smear it along the bridge of your nose. That will make the bony part catch the light and stand out.*

*Put light bits under your eyebrows and another in a half-circle along the bony bit at the top of your cheek.*

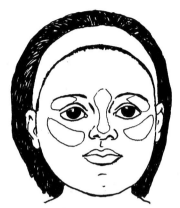

Put light make-up on the bony bits

*Can you see how your face hasn't really changed, but the shape is much clearer?*

*If you have a black skin, the more you lighten the bits that stick out, the more the dark bits will sink in.*

Changing your eyebrows—

Cover your own eyebrows and put new ones in a different place—

...or add some below yours so you look funny

...or change their shape—

**Adding shadows to your face.** If you have a white skin and want to make the bony parts stand out even more, use a face paint or make-up darker than your skin. Fill in the deep hollows on each side of your nose and in your cheeks. The more darkly you colour the shadows, the more the light bits will seem to stick out. Put shadows under your eyes.

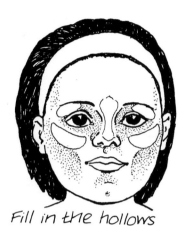

Fill in the hollows with darker make-up

**Ways of making yourself look spooky and frightening.** Shine the torch from below your chin onto your face. Look at the light and dark bits. Now use your make-up to make these clearer.

Fill in different shadows and highlights to look spooky!!

**Making yourself look older.** Screw up your face and look in the mirror. See where the lines appear. Raise your eyebrows so that you get lines on your forehead. If you have white skin, put shadows along these lines. Whatever the colour of your skin, put light lines where the folds of the skin stick out.

Use lines to show wrinkles!!

**Use colours in your make-up.** A tiny dot of red in the corner of your eye beside your nose makes your eyes look very bright. A dark red line round your lips makes the shape clear. Green or blue on your eyelids makes your eyes look clear and interesting.

**Animal make-up.** Think about the shapes and colours of different animals' noses. If you put a darker colour on your nose, it will make it look smaller. If you put on a lighter colour, or white or red, your nose will look bigger.

In the same way, you can change the shape of other parts of your face, just by using light or dark make-up to shadow or highlight.

What about whiskers? You could paint them on. Or use cotton wool, or knitting wool.

Make yourself look like...

A Lion—

A Bear—

A Mouse!

paper cones

*Look at your mask in a mirror. What is it like? Is it happy? Terrifying? Sad? Funny? Wise? Think about the feelings shown in your mask's face.*

A mask is a new face. With it you can change the shape, colour and expression of your face in a moment. It can be very frightening and it can look very kind. Warriors used masks when they went into battle to make themselves look more terrifying. Some helmets are like masks.

Masks that looked like animals were used in dances before the hunters went into the forest. The dance told the hunting story to bring the hunters good luck. Other masks were used in dances which the farmers thought would help the crops to grow.

In the Greek theatre actors wore masks which covered their faces. A sad character would have big staring eyes and a sad mouth, and a funny character would have narrow eyes and a turned-up mouth, as though he was laughing. In the Commedia dell'Arte theatre in Italy in the eighteenth century, each actor wore a 'half-mask'. It covered the top half of their faces and their noses. In the same way as their movements told the audience more about what they were saying, so the mask told the audience more about what sort of character they were playing: Pantaloon, the silly old man, had a long, hooked nose. Harlequin, the naughty servant, had a dark leather mask with a snub nose.

*How does your mask person walk? How does it hold its hands, its shoulders?*

*Show the spirit of the mask in all your movements.*

In Japanese Noh theatre, the girls' parts are played by men with beautiful masks, some of which have been handed down from actor to actor for hundreds of years.

A word of warning. When you learn how to make your mask on the next page, and find out how to use it, be careful. Masks really do change the way you look. They are meant to. But they can also change the way you behave. They are magic in a strange way. If someone asks you to take your mask off, always do it at once. That is an important rule when professional actors are playing with masks. You should obey it too.

On the next page are some ideas for different masks for you to make and use yourself.

When you have made your mask, put it on. Then stand in front of a mirror. Does your face look happy? Do you look terrifying? Or are you sad? Make your body into a shape that seems to go with the mask. How does your mask person walk? How does it hold its hands and shoulders?

Practise walking about and then go back to the mirror and have a long look. Does all of you look as though the spirit of the mask has taken you over and has you in its power? But don't forget. If somebody asks you to take the mask off, do it at once.

**Paper mask.** *You need a sheet of paper, scissors, paints or crayons, and elastic. Cut the shape of mask you want. It could be long, thin and sad, or wide, fat and happy. Anything you like. Paint on the nose, eyes and mouth. You could paint the face bright colours, or stick on silver paper to make it shine. Or glue on coloured tissues to make bits of the mask stick out: a beaky nose, puffy cheeks, bony eyebrows. Cut holes for the eyes and mouth. Thread elastic through small holes on either side of the mask, pass it round the back of your head, tight enough to hold the mask against your face, and knot it.*

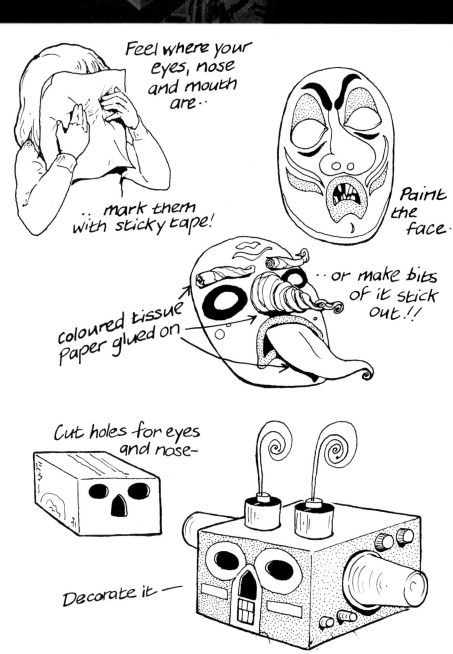

Feel where your eyes, nose and mouth are..

.. mark them with sticky tape!

Paint the face.

coloured tissue paper glued on

.. or make bits of it stick out.!!

Cut holes for eyes and nose-

Decorate it —

**A box mask.** *This is especially good for robots and space travellers. Try sticking on milk-bottle tops to make it glitter. Or paper cups to make strange ears or noses.*

*Add hair or a beard or moustache – made from cotton wool, knitting wool, raffia, or thin strips of foil or paper.*

## A mask like your own face.

*You need tin foil, a mirror, cardboard, sticky tape, papier maché made from tissue paper soaked in flour and water, paint.*

Look in the mirror. Press the tin foil over your face. As soon as you have made the shape of your nose, press two little holes for your nostrils, so you can breathe. Lift it away carefully, holding the edges so that you don't spoil the shape. Fasten it to stiff card with sticky tape. Now lay the papier maché carefully in strips over the tin foil. Put on three or four layers, following the shape and taking care not to damage the foil. Leave it to dry. When it is quite dry and hard, lift it away from the foil. Paint or colour it. Cut holes for the eyes and nose. Thread elastic through small holes on each side of the mask, pass it round the back of your head, and knot it.

## A papier maché half mask.

*Make it in the same way as the full mask, but when the papier maché is still wet, make the nose into all sorts of strange shapes by putting more tissue on it and modelling it just like clay. Cut under cheeks and nose leaving your mouth and chin free.*

1. Press tin foil over your face!

2. Fasten it to card with sticky tape

Put on papier maché in strips

3.

4. Paint it or colour it...

5. Make holes for your eyes and nose

Make the nose into strange shapes

cut under nose and cheeks

People in real life don't just wear clothes to keep
warm. You know how different we look when we dress
up for a special occasion. A football or hockey player
wears the same coloured shirt as the rest of the team. A
policeman wears a uniform. Somebody who wants to
show they are on holiday wears casual clothes.

If you look at books of costume from history you will see that people who had to work in the fields or in the factories wore simple loose clothes that didn't get in the way of their work. Rich people who didn't have to work with their hands usually wore fine clothes with lots of bows and decorations on them.

When you decide on a costume, first think about your character. What does he or she have to do in the play? This will help you to decide what they should wear and how they should behave in the costume.

Long skirts may make you take small steps. Wide sleeves would be nice to show off – so you could carry your arms away from your body. Just as your mask told you to walk in a different way, your costume will tell you to move and behave in a different way. Indian moccasins make you feel able to run and jump and creep quietly. But heavy shoes with heels make you walk carefully and keep to the pavements. An animal costume should make you move like that animal.

A costume in a play tells the audience at once in what period of history the play is set, in which country the characters live, and what sort of life the characters lead.

Think of your new costume for your character as a new skin. You are a completely new person. You can be anything you want to be in your new clothes.

Here's a game using whatever dressing-up clothes you have at home. Put one piece of clothing for each member of the group in the centre of the room. Each person in turn has to run to the pile of clothing, pick one piece, and put it on. Then think of a question that someone wearing that piece of clothing might ask. They must then turn to the person nearest them and ask them that question. The person they speak to picks up another piece of clothing from the pile and answers the question in their new character's voice. Then they in turn ask someone else a question, and the game goes on.

You could play a slightly different game. You each perform some actions which you think the clothes suggest. The next person has to guess who you are.

Dress the characters in your play to suit the sort of people they are. Don't be afraid to experiment. Would it be better if you had a walking stick, a hand bag? Would a hat make your character look more real?

*All you need to create costumes for your plays are some old clothes – even a length of cloth or old sheet. Small strips of cloth can be used as decorations or bows. Use scarves and belts. What about hats?*

*Look hard at the piece of clothing. What does it suggest to you? What kind of material is it – rough and thick, or silky? Brightly coloured, or dull? What kind of person might have worn it? Drape it over yourself and see how it looks. Try wearing it in different ways.*

# Plays for strange faces

On these pages there is a play and some ideas for plays in which the actors can change their faces using make-up or masks; or they can wear costumes. Some of the plays have endings. In others you have to make up your own endings. You could do these plays in any of the ways we have already talked about.

In the first play we have started you off with some dialogue which you could continue. In the other plays you have to make up the dialogue yourselves. Read the stories first, and make up your list of characters.

### The box of woe and joy

*An old man and his wife are gathering firewood in a forest*

**Man**    Come along, wife. Help me to gather firewood. We must warm our old bones in front of a good blaze.

**Woman**    And we must cook ourselves a nice hot stew on the fire. These winter nights are getting colder and colder.

**Man**    Ah, yes – it's bad to be cold and hungry when you are old. But never mind. Work hard! It will warm us.

**Woman**    Work will warm us today, but our fire will both warm and feed us tonight.

**Man**    And your stew will make us strong for more hard work again tomorrow, old lady. That's what life is – work, work, work!

**Woman**    But how terrible it is to have to work so hard every day! My poor back aches and aches!

**Man**    Ah, if only we were rich! If only we were rich!

**Woman**    If we were rich – ah, yes! Then we wouldn't have to crack our bent bones gathering firewood.

**Man**    Look, wife! Look over there! Do you see it?

**Woman**    A box. A golden box! With a painted lid and a silver lock!

**Man**    Bless us! Just come and look at this. I do believe we have found some treasure.

**Woman**    Is it heavy, husband? Do you think it is full of gold?

**Man**    Feel it, wife, feel it! It's full of something.

**Woman**    It is heavy! Can you open the lock? Look, here is a stone. Hammer on the lock with this.

**Man**    There! Ah, good! Now – let us see.

**Woman**    Just imagine that! Jewels! Necklaces! Sapphires! Emeralds, rubies, diamonds and pearls! We are rich!

**Man**    Bless me! And silver chains and golden bracelets! We are rich! But – oh! Suppose the box belongs to someone?

**Woman**    Nonsense! Let us keep it. It must be fairy treasure. Who could possibly lose such a thing in a forest?

**Man**    That's true. You are right! It must be fairy treasure. It must have been left here on purpose, for us to find. But – what's this?

*(Some goblins come creeping on. They creep around the old couple, chanting)*

**Goblins**    They shall find the box,
They shall keep the box.
If they keep the box,
Then woe shall be theirs!

| | |
|---|---|
| | *(The goblins creep away)* |
| **Man** | Am I dreaming? They were wood-goblins, wife! What did they say? Woe shall be ours if we keep the box? |
| **Woman** | Rubbish! You imagined it. |
| | *(Some elves come skipping on. They skip around the old couple, chanting)* |
| **Elves** | They shall find the box,<br>They shall give the box.<br>If they give the box,<br>Then joy shall be theirs! |
| | *(The elves skip away)* |
| **Woman** | Am I enchanted? They were river-elves, husband! What did they say? Joy shall be ours if we give up the box? |
| **Man** | Rubbish! You imagined it. |
| **Woman** | Yes – we shall keep the box. |
| **Man** | Keep the box? Of course we shall keep it! |
| **Woman** | Hush! Someone is coming! Hide the box behind you! |
| | *(An ugly old witch hobbles towards them)* |
| **Witch** | Help an old woman, gentle people! My youth is gone, my beauty is gone, and I am ragged and poor, and hungry and cold. Give me something, I beg you! |
| **Woman** | Go away, old woman! Be off! My youth is gone, too. And my beauty also. How can we help you? We have nothing to give. |
| **Witch** | Please have pity. Have pity on the old and poor! |
| **Man** | Away with you! We are old and poor, too. Why do you come begging to us? We have nothing to spare. |
| **Witch** | Give me my youth and beauty, gentle people! Give them back to me. I left all my youth and beauty in a box. I lost it here, a great, great while ago. |
| **Man** | She's a mad old witch! What a tale! Lost her youth and beauty – in a box, indeed! |
| **Woman** | Go away, you ugly old thing! |
| **Witch** | *(Chanting)*<br>Three warnings they have had!<br>Three chances they have had!<br>Are they good, or are they bad?<br>Shall joy be theirs, or woe so sad? |
| | *(The witch hobbles away)* |
| **Woman** | What did she say? It sounded like a spell. I'm worried, husband. You called the old woman a witch. Do you really think she was? |
| **Man** | Of course not, you silly creature! She's just crazed in the head. She's mad! |
| **Woman** | But she talked of the box. How did she know? Perhaps the box *is* hers. |
| **Man** | Never! How could she be so poor and ragged if all this wealth was really hers? |
| **Woman** | That's true enough. Then she must have been spying on us when we found the box. That's it! That's how she knew about the box. |
| | *(The old people's son, a woodcutter, enters)* |
| **Son** | Come along, mother and father! It will soon be dark, and it's time for us to go home. But, father, what's that you are hiding behind your back? |

Now go on by making up the dialogue yourselves. The son discovers the box. The old couple tell him about the goblins, the elves and the witch. The son says they must find the witch, and all three go off in search.

The goblins appear again, to guide them – or perhaps to tempt them. And the elves appear again, saying the box does indeed belong to the ragged old witch.

The son and his parents find the witch, and the man and his wife say they are sorry. The son gives the box to the witch. When he does so, she changes into a beautiful princess. Perhaps she does that by just taking off a mask.

What happens then? Is the forest changed by magic into a palace? Is there a king and a court? Or is the forest changed into a castle where a wizard lives with goblins? What happens to the old people? And to their son?

## Witches, wizards, warlocks and spells

Boadicea, the proud and powerful queen of an ancient British tribe, was celebrating the Feast of the Old Year with her two daughters and the priests and people of the tribe. It was the night of the year when witches were supposed to appear, if the right spells were said.

The witches do appear, and they are asked to tell the future. One tells the queen her tribe will be attacked and defeated by the Romans. The queen gives a proud reply. Another witch says the Romans will capture the queen, beat her and ill-treat her daughters. Boadicea asks what her revenge will be. A witch says Boadicea will raise an army from two tribes and will lead it to destroy the Roman cities and temples of Colchester and London. But other spirits appear. They say the Romans, in their turn, will take a terrible revenge. Their armies will come again. The Britons will be defeated, and Boadicea and her daughters will take poison and die.

## The huntress and the stag

Artemis, the goddess of wild things and hunting, was in a wood one day with her nymphs, the girl-spirits who attended her. They were making a sacrifice to the sky-god, Zeus, who was the goddess's father.

Actaeon and his followers, who are out hunting, suddenly come upon them by accident. The nymphs tell the hunters to go away, because they are disturbing a holy place, and the goddess must not be seen by men. Actaeon asks who this goddess is and, when he is told, goes to her and boasts that he is a better hunter than she. For this insult, and because of his rough behaviour, Artemis turns Actaeon into a stag, and all his companions into wild animals. The wild animals turn on the stag and kill it.

## A warning – 5,000 years old

A professor and students are digging to see if they can find the tomb of a king of ancient Egypt. They reach the tomb and find it has been closed up with a huge slab of rock. There are some strange letters carved on the rock. They are a curse, which is supposed to fall on anybody who disturbs the sleeping king. The professor and students start to break into the tomb.

Then what happens?

# Feelings, meanings, crowds and fights

What does it feel like to be sad, happy or angry? You may think that is a silly question. You'll probably say, 'I know what it's like because I feel like that often.' But when you are making a play, you have to find out how to show those feelings to other people. In this part of th book we play some games which help us to think about different feelings and how we show them to other peopl

Crowds of people often show their feelings as a grou even more, as if their anger or excitement is catching, like a cold. Sometimes angry feelings can become so strong that a fight starts. In this chapter we learn how to fight so that we show our feelings, but no one is hurt.

When people feel strongly about something they sometimes try to hide it. It can be interesting to guess what it is that they are hiding.

Can you understand what people are feeling even when you can't hear what they are saying? Look at somebody across a room. Observe how they are standing, how they use their hands when they talk. You can often tell what mood they are in. If they are stooping or their heads are hanging down as they talk, perhaps they are frightened. If they wave their hands about a lot, perhaps they are excited. If they keep shifting from foot to foot, perhaps they are worried or nervous.

When making a play we need to show how we are feeling with every bit of our bodies. Here's a game to get you using every part of you to show your feelings.

On a piece of paper write all the parts of the body – head, arms, legs, hands, fingers and so on.

Cut up the paper so that the name of each part of the body is on a different slip of paper. On another piece of paper write all the feelings you can think of. 'Happy', 'sad', 'angry' are usual ones. But think of others as well. 'Jolly' is different from 'happy'. 'Fed up' is different from 'sad'. What about 'jealous', or 'bored', or 'suspicious'? Now cut the paper into slips with a different feeling written on each one.

Place all the 'parts of the body' papers into one tin or hat and all the 'feelings' papers into another. Each person now chooses one piece of paper from the feelings and one piece of paper from the parts of the body.

*Can you understand what someone is feeling even when you can't hear what they are saying? Look at people across the room. Observe how they are standing, how they use their hands, how they hold their heads.*

It is like a lucky dip. You musn't look at the writing on the paper before you pull it out.

You might pick out a 'happy' 'stomach' or 'angry' 'ankles' or 'sad' 'fingers'. Take your partner and decide on a scene to act, using any of the games that you have learnt in this book. But each of you must try to play your character in such a way that the other can guess what bits of paper you picked. Think hard about how the part of the body usually looks. Then think how you might change it to show a different feeling.

When you get very good at playing that game, make it harder. Draw two feelings and two parts of the body.

You might draw a 'tired' 'head' and 'happy' 'feet', or 'bored' 'elbows' and 'worried' 'knees'!

Here's another game about feelings. Think of a simple action, like tying a shoe-lace, or painting a chair. Mime it. Feel the laces between your fingers. Feel the weight of the paint-brush. Make the size of the chair clear. Decide on a feeling you want to show and why you feel like this. Can you now tie that shoe-lace in such a way that your partner knows what you are feeling? Can you tell your partner by the way you put the paint on to the chair whether you are happy or sad? Or that you don't like doing it? Or that you're in a hurry to finish? Think of two or three different feelings and see if you can do exactly the same action in several different ways because you are feeling different each time.

When you become very clever at showing what your character is feeling, it's fun to see if you can show something that your character is trying to hide.

*Show how you are feeling with every part of your body.*

Each choose a partner, and then get into fours. Two of you decide secretly on something to talk about – a television programme or a visit somewhere. Also decide secretly on something that has happened which you won't talk about. Maybe you have had a terrible quarrel. Or one of you has invited the other on a wonderful holiday.

The other pair should now come and listen to you. Talk about the television programme or the visit, but at the same time, without talking about it, try to show in the *way* that you speak to each other what you feel about the person you're talking to. It's quite difficult at first, but keep trying. It's like breaking a code.

Think about the movements you make with your hands. Think of how you stand. Do you face your partner when you talk to them or do you turn away? All these things can signal what you are feeling to someone who is watching you.

Here's a game which can be very funny to watch. First decide who and where you are – perhaps explorers in the Arctic, or a television crew in the Brazilian jungle. Talk to each other about the sorts of things that these people really would talk about in that situation. But at the same time show the people watching your game what your character is secretly feeling. An explorer might say 'Of course I'm not cold!' but might really be feeling 'I wish I'd brought another pair of woolly socks!'

Here is a game which is like talking without words. Choose a nursery rhyme. Don't tell the rest of the group what it is. Recite the nursery rhyme to them, not in proper words, but in nonsense language or sounds.

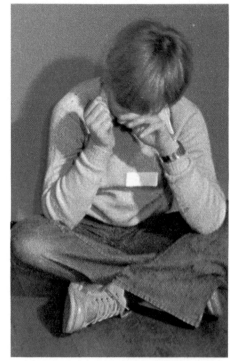

We call it 'gibberish'. Nursery rhymes are good to start with because most people know them and someone guesses what you are saying quite quickly.

When you have played 'nursery rhyme gibberish', take a partner and see whether you can tell your partner a story using nonsense language or gibberish. Ask your partner to tell the same story to you in real words to see how much they have understood. Now change over and let them tell you a story. It's like inventing your own code language. But the *way* that you say things means that other people learn to understand you without actually speaking your language.

*Think of two or three feelings and see if you can do exactly the same action in several different ways because you are showing a different feeling each time.*

*To play the carrying and exchanging game, each pair picks up their object. Really believe in it. How long is it? How heavy? What is its shape? Each pair then carries their object over to the other pair at the same time.*

*Now you have to swap your objects with each other. The first pair passes their object over to the second pair, and at the same time, the second pair passes their object to the first pair. Never let the objects touch the ground. You can all give each other orders about how to grasp the objects, but you must not actually say what they are. You can say all sorts of things like 'quickly, hold this end', or 'mind you don't break the legs', or 'quick it's hot', but you musn't name the objects. After you have exchanged your objects, see if you can guess what has been passed to you.*

*When you become good at the game, choose unusual things to pass to each other, like a giant octopus, or a huge glass tank full of water and fish. Or a live snake. Or an up-rooted tree.*

Do you remember a game you played when you were learning to mime? Two of you decided to carry an object between you in such a way that others could guess what you were carrying. Here's another way to play it. Two pairs of people play it together. In pairs, decide secretly what you are going to carry. It must be big enough to need both of you to carry it. You musn't tell the other pair what it is. Then each pair picks up the object between them and carries it over to the other pair, both pairs moving at the same time. Now swap your objects with each other. The first pair passes their object to the second pair. At the same time the second pair passes their object to the first pair. Never let the objects touch the ground.

You can all give each other orders about how to grasp the objects, but you must not actually say what they are. You can say things like 'quickly, hold this end!' or 'it's hot!' but you must not name the objects. Then you have to guess what has been passed to you.

A crowd in your play, in which everyone feels the same, can help the audience to believe more in what is happening. If a group of people are all suddenly very frightened at the same time, it can create a scary mood.

Play this game. Stand in a circle, and start counting together from one to ten. Count a little quieter on each number so that by the time you reach ten you are whispering. Listen very carefully to everyone else. All speak together so that it sounds like just one person.

Now do the opposite. Start very quietly with a whisper at number one and slowly get louder and louder until you are shouting the number ten.

Crowds are often made up of people saying or doing different things at the same time. If you are in a crowd scene, make up something real to say, don't just talk nonsense. This game helps you to get the feeling of a real crowd, all of whom have something real to say.

Divide the group into two halves. Choose a partner from the other half of the group. Each go to the opposite side of the room from each other and face each other. Now everyone must try to have a conversation with their partner across the room. It will get very noisy. Concentrate hard on talking to your partner. Sometimes it becomes so noisy that you can't shout above the din. Then try talking quite quietly, but very clearly. It can become possible to hear each other again.

Remember that the crowd in your play must not make so much noise that you can't hear what other characters say. Also, crowds who whisper to each other are sometimes very strange and create a wonderful mood.

*Learning to fall without hurting yourself is the most important thing in stage fighting. You must begin with that. Practise it over and over again. The more you do it, the easier it will be.*

1. Drop to one knee...

2. Then sit down sideways

Without using your hands!!

Fights are about feelings too – anger, or wanting to hurt someone. They can also be about being frightened and defending yourself. You have to show all these things by your body movements. You have to show pain, for example, without really being hurt.

But fighting in plays can be dangerous. The first thing to learn is how to do it safely. No one must get hurt, but you all have to act as though you are hurting each other. Learning to fall without hurting yourself is the most important thing. You must begin with that.

Never try to practise stage fights when you are cold, or tired. You must go right back to the beginning. Do you remember how you did the warm-up at the beginning of this book? Do the same now. Have a big stretch. Shake your hands until you feel your fingers are going to drop off. Shake your feet until your toes tingle.

Find a space, not too close to anyone else or too near the walls. Stretch out all around you as far as you can reach, in every direction. Lie along the floor as though you are the hands of a clock, to make sure that you won't bump into anyone else when you fall.

Now is the time to learn how to fall properly. Practise dropping down onto one knee. That's all you have to do.

When you have got used to that, try this. Drop down onto one knee and then sit down sideways without using your hands. Do that a few times until it feels easy. Try sitting down on both sides, to the left and to the right.

Think of your knee as number 1, your hip as number 2.

The next stage of breaking your fall is to put your hand out on the floor. Your hand is number 3. Your elbow drops to the floor next. It is number 4, and then your shoulder is number 5. Each part of your body which has a number must drop to the floor in that order. This way you won't hit your head and hurt yourself. Do it over and over again. The more you do it, the more relaxed you will become.

3. Break your fall by putting out your hand...

4. Lower your elbow to the ground

5. Drop onto your

shoulder!

**Punches.** *Close both fists. Aim your punch so that it stops before you touch your partner's body. At the exact same time, hit yourself with the inside of your other fist on the upper part of your chest or shoulder.*

**Slaps.** *Always slap the face on the side furthest away from the audience. The person who is being slapped brings the opposite hand up to their cheek as if to defend it. The attacker actually slaps their hand and not their face!*

*Or you can aim to miss the face. The person who is being attacked jerks their head away from the slap at the moment it would have landed. At the same instant, they clap their hands together.*

Here's a good game for learning stage fighting. Blow up some balloons. Choose a partner who is about your own size. One person hits the other with the balloon. The other one pretends to be hit with a stick or an iron bar and falls over or clutches an arm or leg as though in pain. Take it in turns to hit each other. It isn't actually necessary for the attacker to hit the defender at all hard, but the defender has to look as though the blows are hard and hurting them quite a lot.

If you make too much of a fuss when you fall over it will be funny. That's useful. Not all fights in plays are serious; some are meant to be funny. But they are just as difficult. And you have to be just as careful not to get hurt by making sure you fall in the right way.

Try different ways of hitting with the balloon. Hit your partner on different parts of the body. Try different ways of falling.

Another good way to prepare for stage fighting is to build yourself an obstacle course – over chairs, under tables, behind desks. Go over your obstacle course in a number of different ways – gently and carefully, timidly, boldly, clumsily, or daintily – like a dancer.

Fights are as much about feelings as everything else in your play. Not everyone fights in the same way.

58

"Hair Pulling" —
Put your clenched fist on your partner's head

The victim holds the fist against the head. So really no hair is held!

Ouch!!

Holding hands

Sometimes people are forced to fight when they don't want to. Others choose to fight. Some people are bullies and only enjoy fighting people smaller than themselves, so they can win. Some people fight fairly and would not attack someone from behind. Others are dishonest in their fights and try to trick their opponents.

There are many ways of playing your fight scene. Why does the fight start? Give your fight a beginning, a middle section, and an end.

Can you show those who are watching how stupid and wasteful fighting can be? Do you want to show that one person is in the right and the other wrong? A famous playwright and theatre director once gave all the soldiers in his battle scene white faces because he wanted to show that everyone in war is frightened.

Here is how to 'fight' safely without weapons.

The important thing about fighting with hands, fists and feet is to make the noises of the blows, and to see the behaviour of the person who is hit, without the blow ever actually landing on that person's body. It's just like mime. You have to make it *sound* and look as though you have punched or slapped someone without actually touching them. Your partner must of course double up and cry out by letting their breath out quickly.

Even paper weapons, like swords and daggers, can hurt you. So it is important to learn how to use them safely.

Hold your sword like this....

When you defend yourself in sword-fighting, you 'parry' the attacker's sword-blade. This means that you stop the attacker's blade with your own sword, so that the attacker's blade ends up pointing away from your head and body, instead of straight at it.

attackers

Parrying to your left    Parrying to your right

defenders

Defending yourself by parrying.

Low parry to the right

Low parry to the left

Parry to defend your head

High parry to the left

High parry to the right

Here are some attack movements for you to practise. Make each movement very clear, so your partner can see where you are aiming to hit. Always try to hit your partner with the side of the sword, not the point.

Whatever weapons you fight with, always use the positions of attack and defence shown on these pages. When you have practised them, experiment with the order of your movements. Break your fight up into little sections so that you can remember it. Don't forget that real fighters will get tired, so your stage fight could have pauses, while the fighters rest or circle each other slowly, looking for a chance to attack. But at the beginning, when they are fresh, there will probably be very quick sections.

Remember that in all fights there has to be a loser. So take it in turns!

Attacking different parts of the body. Notice how the defender parries the blows, or "cuts".

Low cut to defender's right side

Low cut to defender's left side

Cut to head

High cut to defender's right side

High cut to defender's left side

# Plays to make from stories

Here are two stories from which you can make plays. The first is about pirates. The characters are: a pirate captain, the ship's mate, some officers and the crew. The play takes place on board ship. You might want to mark out the size and shape of the ship's deck and decide at which end of the ship the crew live, and which part is used by the officers. You might also want to mark where masts and ropes are.

## Pirates in a pickle

It was a fine sunny day, and a fresh, light breeze drove the pirate ship fast through the water. You would have thought it was a perfect day to be afloat in the middle of the calm, blue sea. But something was wrong. There on the deck, all by himself, stood the pirate captain. He looked miserable. Then he looked more and more miserable. And then he started to cry!

Although he was a pirate captain he was not very fierce. And he certainly was not very cunning or clever. If you could have seen him crying you would have felt quite sorry for him. The mate did, when he came out on deck. You could not say the mate was very fierce, either. He just liked everything to be quiet and peaceful, so he was sorry when he saw his captain crying. He put an arm round the captain's shoulders and tried to comfort him!

It took the captain some time to get his story out. He kept on saying the crew would be very angry, and he didn't see how he could tell them the truth – and, oh, wasn't it a shame and a pity, and whatever should he do? It was all very mysterious, and the mate had to try very hard to help the captain to explain what was troubling him.

In the end the captain did. Though they had been sailing for many, many weeks, in search of an island where some treasure was buried, they had really been wasting their time. The captain had promised all the officers and crew they would be rich, but now he would have to turn the ship round and go back home and start all over again. The mate had looked forward to being rich, so he was very disappointed to hear this. But why had their voyage been a waste of time? Why did they have to go back home and start all over again?

At this, the captain started sniffing and dabbing at his eyes once more. They could never find the treasure, they could never find the island where it was buried, because he had just discovered he had left his treasure-map at home!

A pretty story to tell the crew! Yes, the crew would indeed be angry! Then the mate and the captain started to frighten each other – what if the crew kill us, or make us walk the plank? They'll put us in irons! They'll cast us adrift on a raft! They trembled to think of what the crew might do to them.

Of course, the captain was almost as afraid to tell the officers. But the mate called for them to come on deck, and one by one they appeared. From the look on the captain's face they knew something was wrong! However, they were used to that because the captain had got them into lots of muddles before. Had the ship sprung a leak? Were they lost? Had the ship's cat had kittens? Had rats chewed the sails? Was there a storm coming? What *was* the matter? First they asked each other, then they looked nervously at the captain, and then they looked at each other again and began to ask more questions.

But the captain and the mate just shook their heads dolefully. The mate called for silence, and the captain told his story. Well of course the officers were as angry as you would expect. What a captain! What a ship! What a life! What a waste of time! All those weeks and weeks of sailing! For nothing!

Then the officers thought of what the crew might do, and very quickly they became nearly as frightened as the captain. But the captain hastily promised he would double the officers' share of the treasure – when they found it – if they would promise to take his side against the crew. So the officers agreed, and the crew were called. They came chattering up on deck, wondering why they had been called away from their work. The mate shouted for silence. The officers just looked at one another and got safely out of the way behind the captain.

The captain shifted from foot to foot. He ummed and ah-ed and stuttered. But slowly – very slowly – he managed to break the bad news to them. For a moment there was a very strange sort of silence. Then the crew started hissing and boo-ing. What! Sailing all this way for nothing? Wasting their lives with a captain who didn't know his business! They must have been mad to trust their lives to him!

First the sailors suspected it was a trick. Then they told each other that the captain had not *really* said what they thought he had. So they sent some sailors to ask him questions. Surely he had some idea where the treasure was? Why not sail on and search for the island? Surely that was better than giving up? But the captain just looked very ashamed, and then he looked very silly. And the more the sailors watched him, the sillier he seemed. Getting them all this way for nothing! They'd be better off if they chose a captain of their own – someone who could lead them to search for the treasure, even without a map.

And so they muttered and they grumbled. And one or two began to say that perhaps they should kill the captain and take over the ship. The other sailors were so angry they would have listened to any plan. And so they all turned and looked at the officers, because they would have to get rid of them, too!

The officers nervously drew their swords. They could guess what the crew were saying! And then, without warning, some of the crew rushed at the captain and the officers. Within a moment, all the rest had joined in. Some fought with weapons, some wrestled, some fought with their fists. Slowly the officers were forced back, and it looked as if all the nasty things the captain and the mate had feared might come true.

But, suddenly, there was a distant *boom!* The fight stopped. They all froze where they were. There was another *boom!* In a split second the officers and crew were rushing about, their fight forgotten. There were cries of 'It's a ship!', 'They're firing on us!', 'It's the Navy!' and 'We'll all be hanged!'.

The mate yelled orders to crowd on more sail. The captain hopped about and told them to run the Jolly Roger up the mainmast. The officers gave orders for the crew to trim the foresail, hoist the topsail, steer down the wind and run for it, clear the decks for action, run out the guns, fetch up the ammunition, and to haul on this rope and let go that one.

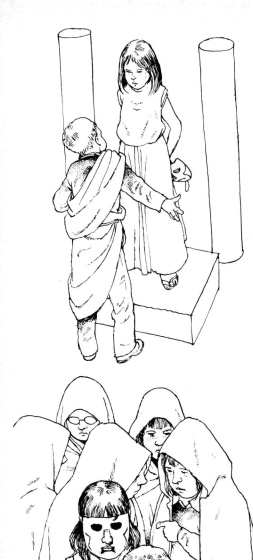

All together, they dashed and scurried about in a furious fever of work and worry to escape from the guns of the Navy.

The captain and the mate walked round and said the crew were all jolly good lads. Some of the crew shook their fists at the Navy ship in the distance. But one or two shook their fists at the captain and said that, later on, when they were not so busy, they meant to finish the little talk they had been having with him and his officers!

Why not make up a second scene to act in the same way? The pirates might discover the ship that was chasing them was not the Navy. Who is it? What happens next? Do they capture the second ship in hand-to-hand fighting? Are they defeated?

## The journey of Aeneas

After the Greeks conquered the city of Troy, Aeneas, one of the heroes who had fought to save his city, wandered for many years until he came to a temple of the sun god. In the temple he found a wise woman, a prophetess called a sibyl.

Aeneas begs the woman to help him. He wants to visit the Underworld, the land of the dead, so that he can ask his dead father for advice. The sibyl says it will be hard for the living to go there, but she will ask the god for permission to take him to the place where the dead souls live.

As she speaks, the sibyl, by putting on a mask, becomes the god Apollo himself. Now she speaks in the god's voice. The god gives his permission, so the sibyl, in the form of the god, takes Aeneas to a secret place that leads to an underground river. There, a ghostly ferryman is waiting. His work is to ferry dead souls from this world to the Underworld.

As Charon, the ferryman, takes Aeneas and the god across the river, the murmuring souls of the people of the Underworld gather on the far bank to meet them. Aeneas recognises some of them, and remembers how they died in the siege of Troy and when the Greeks burnt the city. They ask him if he, too, is dead. But the god explains their journey and asks where they will find the soul of Aeneas's father. The others point, and the soul of the father advances towards them.

Father and son greet each other. Aeneas asks his father what work he should do in the world, and what his fate will be, now that he is a wanderer with no homeland. The father says that his son will be the founder of a great state called Rome, which will become the centre of an empire that will rule the world. A sigh rises from the souls around them.

His father goes, and Aeneas and the god return, amid the wails of the dead souls, who reach out to touch them. Aeneas kneels to the god. The god tells him he will forget his visit to the Underworld, as if it were a dream, but he will always remember what fame awaits him in the future.

Then the god becomes the wise woman, the sibyl, once more. She wakes, as if she has been deeply asleep. Aeneas rubs his eyes, and thanks her for her help. She says she has given him no help, she just closed her eyes and the god came into her head. If Aeneas has been helped by the god she knows nothing about it. She smiles at Aeneas, and tells him to go out into the world and meet his fortune – whatever that may be.

# Stage, props, lights and sound

By now you may have decided that you want to put on one of your plays for other people to watch – perhaps for your friends or your family, or even for another class at school. In this chapter we explore different things you might want to think about in preparing your play.

You may want to put the play on just as you are, without costume or make-up, scenery or props, and without preparing much beforehand. Or you may feel like trying out some scenery, and experimenting with making and using furniture and props. If you do, there are some ideas in this chapter which may help you.

Present your play in any way that suits you, the play and your audience best. Where will you act it? Where will you seat your audience? You could even do it out of doors. Where does the action in your play take place? You could use scenery to help show this. What about making and arranging some? And do you need props for the play? Perhaps you'll want to make or improvise some from materials you can find easily.

As you can see there could be a great many jobs to do and it will help you if you plan a bit in advance, try different things out and choose which ones you will use.

There are many ways to create the setting for your play. First think about what sort of 'theatre' you want. Perhaps you think of a theatre stage as being like a picture frame. You imagine plush red velvet curtains and lots of decoration round the picture. But this is not the only sort of theatre. Through the ages theatres have been many different shapes. Indeed throughout history and in the present day plays have been performed in places that were not built as theatres at all.

In the Greek Theatre the audience sat round in a semi-circle with the actors and the chorus in the centre of the 'horse-shoe'. In the Middle Ages, plays were acted on high carts pulled through the streets. The scenery was just a back-cloth, painted or sewn, and hung at the back of the cart.

During the reign of Queen Elizabeth I, the first theatres to be built in England were in the open air. A roof covered the actors, but not the audience. Most of the audience had no seats. Performances had to be given when it was light in the afternoon.

In the seventeenth century, plays were put on in indoor tennis courts until people began to build theatres. This was when scenery was first used. In order to hide the actors waiting to come on stage and to hide the ropes and pulleys which lowered the scenery from above or pulled it on from the side, they put up screens and so made the 'picture-frame' stage.

*Here are a few suggestions for different ways of seating your audience and placing your stage. The stage could be any shape you like, and you can seat your audience round the acting area in any way you choose. If there are doors, you could use them to get on and off the stage.*

Use the end of a room for your stage —

··· or use the corner ··

Act your play against a wall and seat your audience
in front of you or on three sides of you...

... or act your play in the middle of the room
with your audience all around you!!

Where does your play take place? This is called the 'setting'. Outdoors? In a garden? A forest? On a hillside? By the sea?

Or will you set it indoors – a home, shop, or a place of work? In films, plays can take place in 'locations', that is, in real places. A scene can be filmed in a real field or street. But in your plays you have to give an idea of where your play takes place, so that the audience can imagine it too.

Here are different ways it could be done. Paint life-sized pictures on large sheets of paper and put them up round your stage. Or you can use shapes (like boxes), or drape material and use colours to give the idea of your location. Or again, you could cut shapes in stiff card (a house roof, for example) and prop them up on your stage. Or you can leave your stage quite bare, and leave it all to the imagination!

It may help you to start by making a model of how you want to set your play.

Think about the characters in your plays. What sort of lives do they lead? What kind of furniture would they have and what are you going to use? How do you want to place the furniture in your set? You could use little pieces of furniture (like doll's house furniture) in your model. Or use small boxes such as match boxes and move them around the model to see how they look. Your audience will want to see the faces of the actors as much as possible, so place your furniture in such a way that when the characters sit down, they face the audience. Try not to put the furniture in a straight line, but make interesting shapes. Leave room for the actors to move around it. It is a good idea to put chairs in groups with big spaces in between.

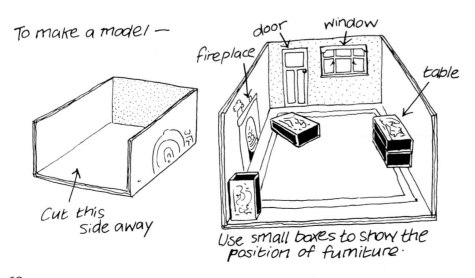

To make a model –

Cut this side away

fireplace

door    window

table

Use small boxes to show the position of furniture.

You need a large cardboard box. Cut away one side, so you can look straight at the remaining sides. This leaves you three sides to paint on, depending on the shape of your stage. Or if your play has several scenes, try painting each side of the box with the setting for a different scene.

You may all have different ideas. Why don't several of you make your own models, and then you could all choose which one of them to use.

68

*Paint life-sized pictures on large sheets of paper and put them up round your stage. You could paint both sides and simply turn the paper round when you want to change the setting.*

Make interesting shapes with your furniture. Leave room for actors to move around.

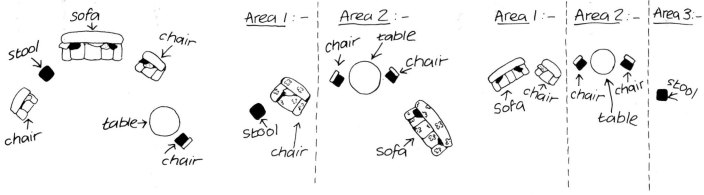

Use the whole stage · · · ·

Put furniture for different scenes in different areas · · · ·

Use tables and chairs and turn them into other things.

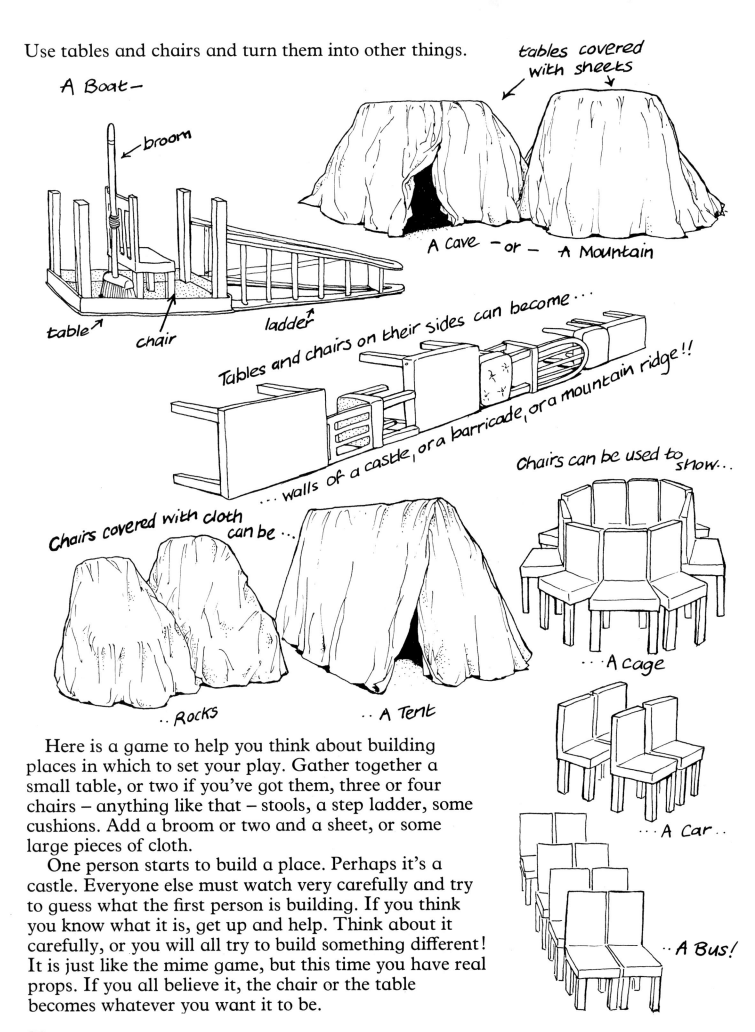

A Boat—

broom

table↗

chair

ladder↗

tables covered with sheets

A Cave — or — A Mountain

Tables and chairs on their sides can become...

... walls of a castle, or a barricade, or a mountain ridge!!

Chairs covered with cloth can be...

.. Rocks

.. A Tent

Chairs can be used to show...

... A Cage

... A Car..

.. A Bus!

Here is a game to help you think about building places in which to set your play. Gather together a small table, or two if you've got them, three or four chairs – anything like that – stools, a step ladder, some cushions. Add a broom or two and a sheet, or some large pieces of cloth.

One person starts to build a place. Perhaps it's a castle. Everyone else must watch very carefully and try to guess what the first person is building. If you think you know what it is, get up and help. Think about it carefully, or you will all try to build something different! It is just like the mime game, but this time you have real props. If you all believe it, the chair or the table becomes whatever you want it to be.

*If you want to try making your own props, collect these kinds of things—you never know how you might think of using them : card and paper ; tin foil or metallic paper like toffee wrappings ; wrappings from chocolate biscuits ; string ; sweet containers ; plastic bottles ; milk bottle tops and other bottle tops ; tin cans ; jars and their lids ; old buckets and bowls ; beads ; old bits of chain ; safety pins. . .*

*Decorate your props by painting, colouring, or sticking things on to them.*

Earlier we played a game where you imagined simple props, like a broom or a hair brush to be other things. Think about your props now in the same way. Turn the objects you have into anything you want, just by imagining it, and then using them to show what they are. Play the prop games.

Or you could make props. With a few pieces of card, some silver foil, string, glue and paints or crayons, you could make all kinds of things.

First think of the jobs your character will be doing during a scene. It is interesting to watch people doing or making something while they talk, for example. Will your character be using tools? A spade, perhaps, or a bucket or other containers? Using a walking stick or magic wand? Perhaps your scene takes place in a kitchen or other part of a house. Do you need cooking pans, bowls and plates? Paper flowers in a vase?

First collect all the bits and pieces you will need: paper, cardboard, scissors, glue, paint, paint-brushes, crayons, felt tip pens. You may need to make things look like metal: use kitchen foil, milk bottle tops, or silver paint. If you want it to look like wood, dip a dry paint brush in rather dry brown water paint and drag it across the surface of the paper or cardboard. Keep the brush dry and do it very lightly, and use only a very little paint at a time. If you want a rough surface to your props, like tree bark or rough wood, crinkle up tissue paper and glue it to the surface.

*Paper, card and paper cups can be used to make all kinds of things — a fan, paper flowers, bowls and plates, weapons. . .*

*If you need your prop to be quite strong, try sticking several layers of card together to strengthen it.*

*Here are some props to give you a few ideas. Experiment with making others.*

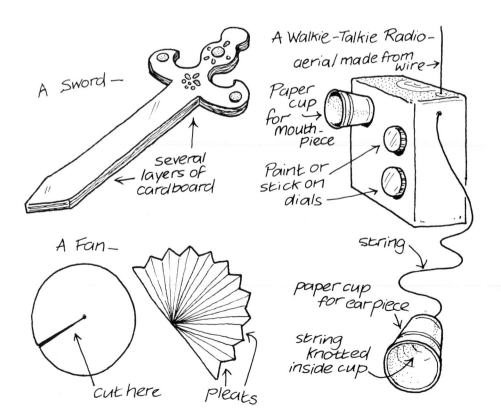

A Sword —

several layers of cardboard

A Walkie-Talkie Radio-
aerial made from wire →

Paper cup for mouth-piece →

Paint or stick on dials —

string

paper cup for earpiece

string knotted inside cup

A Fan —

cut here

pleats

You can use old plastic washing-up liquid bottles for all sorts of things. Stick two together and you've got a telescope with an eye piece at one end. Cut the top off the other end, stick cellophane paper over it and you've got the magnifying glass at the other end. Cut the bottle half way down, to form a long cup, put a piece of thin stick through the bottom and make a base out of the lid of a screw-top jar. Now you have a drinking goblet.

Do you see how props are made – not just from one thing but by sticking lots of different bits and pieces together? Think of the shape you need. Think of the things you can find around the house or at school that are the right shape. Then cut, stick things on, or paint them, to make the prop you want. There are lots of books you can look at to see what objects looked like in the olden days. Your school library will have some.

Sometimes it is interesting to make your props very large, so that characters in your play look much smaller, or like children. Or make them very tiny so that your characters look like giants. You can do plays like 'Jack and the Beanstalk' or 'Gulliver's Travels', in which people are different sizes, by using the same shaped prop twice, one very large, one very small, and the audience will believe that the actors are changing size. Try all sorts of things out, and choose which ones will work best. Then look back at some of the prop mimes and story games in this book. Play them again. If you believe in your prop, your audience will too.

*With plastic washing-up liquid bottles, or decorated bottles, jars and cans, you can make all kinds of other things.*

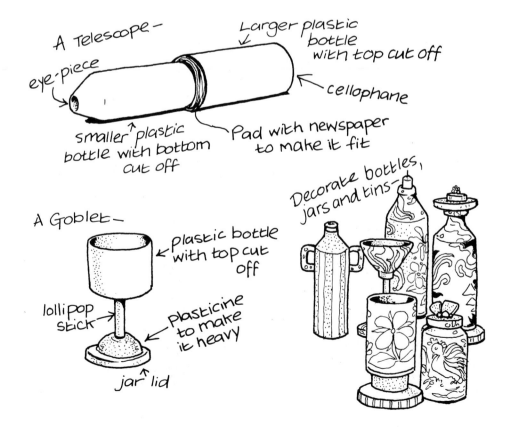

A Telescope —

eye-piece

Larger plastic bottle with top cut off

cellophane

smaller plastic bottle with bottom cut off

Pad with newspaper to make it fit

A Goblet —

plastic bottle with top cut off

lollipop stick

plasticine to make it heavy

jar lid

Decorate bottles, jars and tins —

Try some sound effects. You could make the audience believe there are all sorts of things happening off-stage as well as on it! Find out what kinds of sounds you can make with ordinary household objects. See if you can find a way to make weather noises – wind or rain or thunder. The sound of horses' hooves. Slamming doors. A crash. Something breaking. A fire.

There are some ideas on this page.

You can have a record player at the side of the stage and choose music which helps the mood of your play. Or if some of you can play musical instruments, what about using them? Try drum rolls when something exciting is about to happen, or to accompany a procession, or a fight.

If you have a tape recorder, you can prepare your sound effects first, and then add them to the play.

*Find out what kinds of noises you can make with household objects. Try out the sound of tin cans and bottles, for example. Try out different surfaces of wood and other materials. What sounds can you make with your mouth, or with your hands or feet? Experiment.*

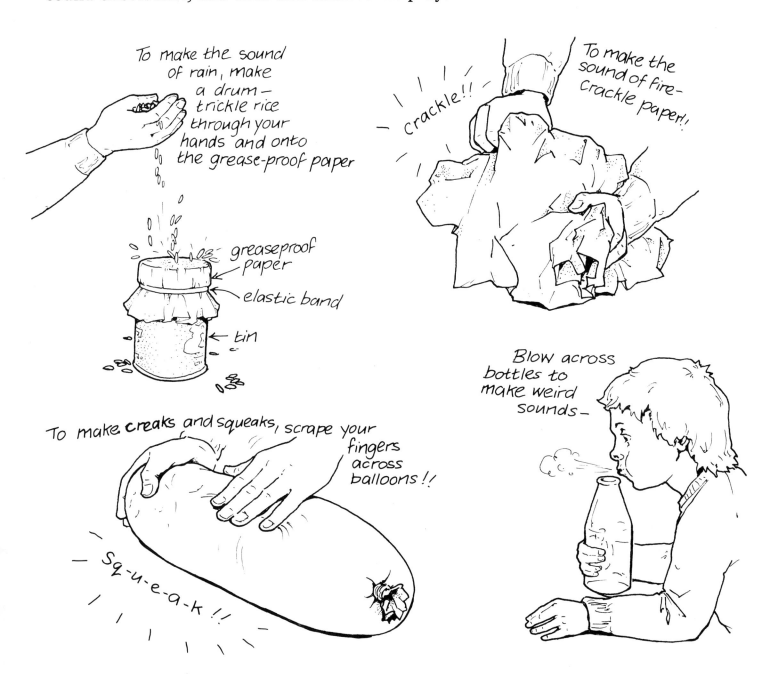

To make the sound of rain, make a drum – trickle rice through your hands and onto the grease-proof paper

greaseproof paper

elastic band

tin

— crackle!!

To make the sound of fire - Crackle paper!!

To make creaks and squeaks, scrape your fingers across balloons!!

— Sq-u-e-a-k!!

Blow across bottles to make weird sounds –

Record yourselves making crowd noises. Or record cars in the street. Or people running up stairs. In this way you can often make it seem as though there are many more people in your play than you and your friends.

Think about how you will light your play. The audience will want to see the actors' faces as much as possible, so position the actors so that the light falls on them most of the time.

If you are doing your play during the day, do you want to draw the curtains and make the room dark? What about using torchlight to make interesting effects – to cast shadows or to light only part of the stage, while everything else is left in darkness.

Or start your play in complete darkness and have someone switch on the light just at the moment when the performance begins.

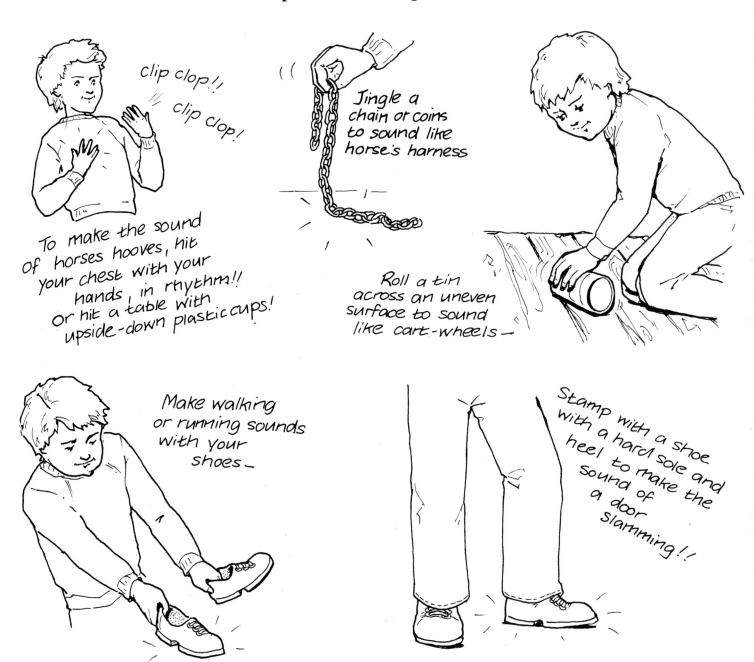

clip clop!! clip clop!

To make the sound of horses hooves, hit your chest with your hands, in rhythm!! Or hit a table with upside-down plastic cups!

Jingle a chain or coins to sound like horse's harness

Roll a tin across an uneven surface to sound like cart-wheels –

Make walking or running sounds with your shoes –

Stamp with a shoe with a hard sole and heel to make the sound of a door slamming!!

When you are getting your play ready to perform, it may help you to plan everything first, and make sure there is someone in your group to do each job. Here are some ideas about the jobs you could give out. First of all, find someone who is going to be in charge of putting up any scenery, and putting the furniture in position. Someone will need to collect any props and put them ready before the performance. Perhaps you'd like to have someone who makes sure all the actors are ready to begin. And someone else who knows when any sound or light effects should be done, and makes sure they happen. This person might find it helpful to write down all the things that should happen, and when. Perhaps you have all decided to write down the dialogue of your play in a play 'script'. You could add to this script all the notes about sound effects, or movements or lights. If you have a script which you all want to remember, you will probably need someone who always has a copy of it, and can remind or 'prompt' anyone who forgets their words during the performance.

You may need another person to switch the lights on and off or to shine the torches, and someone to make the sound effects. And what about a person to look after the costumes during the play, help people change, check and repair their make-up, if they have any?

Then there is the audience to take care of. You will need to show the audience where to sit, if they are just sitting cross-legged on the floor, or arrange cushions or chairs for them.

You could make a programme with the names of everyone who has helped to make the play, the name of the play and a few details about where it takes place, and when.

Perhaps you're going to provide refreshments for your audience, and you will want to get these ready so you can bring them on the moment there is a break in your performance.

Whatever jobs you feel you need to do, you should all get together at the beginning and decide how, and who will do it. Putting on a play well is about working together as a very good team.

*You could add notes to your play script about how you want to perform your play. Write all the sound effects down in a long list, and all the light effects in a separate list. Then number them in the order they happen in the play. The signal to make a sound or light effect is called a 'cue'. So, for example, the sound of lightning might be sound cue 3, and the flash of lightning might be light cue 7. In the margin of your script you write 'go sound cue 3' and 'go light cue 7' when you want the lightning to happen.*

MOVES

Ann and Selina to front of stage

Ainsley, Mark to centre stage

Gilbert, Ann, Jennifer, Timothy to centre stage

76

| LIGHTING CUES | SOUND CUES | This is how your script with notes on it might look. |
|---|---|---|

<table>
<tr><td>(Stand by cue 22)</td><td>(Stand by cue 12)</td><td></td><td></td></tr>
<tr><td>(Stand by cue 23)</td><td>(Stand by Cue 13)</td><td>Child</td><td>And gloomy.</td></tr>
<tr><td></td><td></td><td>Child</td><td>And cold.</td></tr>
<tr><td></td><td></td><td>Child</td><td>Oh, miss – do you think it's haunted?</td></tr>
<tr><td></td><td></td><td>Teacher</td><td>Haunted? Don't be silly! Now, what about this game? Let's play something to pass the time.</td></tr>
<tr><td></td><td>GO cue 12 ———</td><td></td><td>(There is a huge, long crash of thunder. They fall silent</td></tr>
<tr><td></td><td>GO cue 13 ———</td><td></td><td>as the wind roars again and then dies down)</td></tr>
<tr><td>GO cue 22 ———</td><td></td><td>Child</td><td>I don't like it here!</td></tr>
<tr><td></td><td></td><td>Child</td><td>Nor do I!</td></tr>
<tr><td>(Stand by cue 24)</td><td>(Stand by cue 14)</td><td>Child</td><td>I hate thunder!</td></tr>
<tr><td></td><td></td><td>Child</td><td>Perhaps this is a haunted house!</td></tr>
<tr><td></td><td></td><td>Child</td><td>Oh, miss. Tell us a story – tell us a ghost story!</td></tr>
<tr><td></td><td>(Stand by cue 15)</td><td>Child</td><td>Go on, miss. Tell us a story about a haunted house.</td></tr>
<tr><td></td><td>(Stand by cue 16)</td><td>Child</td><td>Like this one.</td></tr>
<tr><td></td><td></td><td>Child</td><td>It's gone dark! Why's it gone dark?</td></tr>
<tr><td>GO cue 23 ———</td><td></td><td>Teacher</td><td>It's those black thunder clouds.</td></tr>
<tr><td></td><td></td><td>Child</td><td>It always goes dark in a storm.</td></tr>
<tr><td></td><td>GO cue 14 ———</td><td></td><td>(There is another thunder crash, and more wind)</td></tr>
<tr><td>GO cue 24 ———</td><td></td><td>Child</td><td>Bang! Crash-bang-crash!</td></tr>
<tr><td></td><td></td><td>Teacher</td><td>Sit down quietly! It'll be over soon and then we can leave.</td></tr>
<tr><td></td><td>GO cue 15 ———</td><td></td><td>(There is a rumble of thunder. During the next few lines</td></tr>
<tr><td></td><td>GO cue 16 ———</td><td></td><td>the wind dies into the background)</td></tr>
<tr><td></td><td></td><td>Teacher</td><td>There! That thunder was much farther away.</td></tr>
<tr><td></td><td></td><td>Child</td><td>It's still raining, though. You can hear it.</td></tr>
<tr><td></td><td></td><td>Child</td><td>Come on, miss – tell us a ghost story!</td></tr>
<tr><td></td><td></td><td>Children</td><td>Yes, miss, please!</td></tr>
<tr><td></td><td></td><td>Teacher</td><td>All right. But first, why don't we eat our lunch here?</td></tr>
<tr><td></td><td></td><td>Children</td><td>I'm starving! What's there to eat, miss?<br>(They unpack their basket)</td></tr>
<tr><td></td><td></td><td>Teacher</td><td>You two, hand things round, and then, while you're eating, I can tell you a story.</td></tr>
<tr><td></td><td></td><td>Child</td><td>A ghost story, miss. About a haunted house.</td></tr>
<tr><td></td><td></td><td>Teacher</td><td>Settle down. I'll think of something.<br>(The children hand round food and drink)</td></tr>
<tr><td></td><td></td><td>Child</td><td>Come on, miss. Once upon a time there was a haunted house.</td></tr>
<tr><td></td><td>(Stand by cue 17)</td><td>Teacher</td><td>(Starting the story, helped by some of the children)<br>Yes, once upon a time there was a haunted house. . .</td></tr>
<tr><td></td><td></td><td>Child</td><td>And some children had to shelter there. . .</td></tr>
<tr><td></td><td></td><td>Child</td><td>From a terrible storm. . .</td></tr>
<tr><td></td><td></td><td>Child</td><td>And the lightning flashed and the thunder rolled. . .</td></tr>
<tr><td></td><td></td><td>Teacher</td><td>But no one was frightened. They were far too sensible. And, of course, they did not know that the house was haunted. . .</td></tr>
<tr><td></td><td></td><td>Child</td><td>But, suddenly, there was a terrible noise. . .</td></tr>
<tr><td></td><td>GO cue 17 ———</td><td></td><td>(Just at that moment there IS a terrible noise! There is a tremendous rattling crash, like a big piece of furniture falling over. They all stop and listen)</td></tr>
<tr><td></td><td></td><td>Teacher</td><td>Whatever was that?</td></tr>
<tr><td></td><td></td><td>Child</td><td>It was up there! Upstairs!<br>(They huddle together and look up)</td></tr>
<tr><td></td><td></td><td>Child</td><td>It sounded like something being knocked over.</td></tr>
<tr><td></td><td></td><td>Child</td><td>Or like a big picture falling down!</td></tr>
</table>

# A play with a script

This play could be acted using properties, costume, and perhaps a bit of scenery and some sound effects and so on. Of course, you could also do it quite simply, without any of those things, and still have just as much fun with it.

**The sailing of the Ark:** a comedy
The characters:
**Mrs Noah**
**Mr Noah,** who is patient, gentle and a bit forgetful
**Japheth, Ham, Shem,** the sons of Mr and Mrs Noah
**Three girls,** the wives of the sons
**Neighbours**

*The play starts with a loud hammering that comes from offstage where, unseen, Mr Noah is building the Ark. Just before the noise stops, Mrs Noah enters. She is carrying a chair. She puts it near some other furniture that is already piled on the stage*

| | |
|---|---|
| **Mrs Noah** | Oh, just listen! My head will split! Is he never going to be finished? *(The three sons enter, each with something from their house, which he piles with the rest)* |
| **Japheth** | What's the matter, mother? |
| **Mrs Noah** | It's your father. All that hammering! He said that boat of his was finished. |
| **Ham** | It is, very nearly. That's why father told us to bring the furniture from the house. |
| **Shem** | And it's not a boat, mother, it's an Ark. |
| **Mrs Noah** | Well it looks like a boat to me. |
| **Ham** | Ah, but this is a boat we can live in. Cheer up, mother! We'll be all right. You'll see. |
| **Japheth** | We've got all your favourite bits of furniture. You'll enjoy it. |
| **Mrs Noah** | What, with all those animals? |
| **Japheth** | Oh! I forgot! Father told me to bring those birds – those two doves we caught yesterday. I'll get them. *(He goes)* |
| **Mrs Noah** | Now it's doves! Whatever does your father want doves for? |
| **Shem** | It's all right, mother. Just leave it to father. |
| **Mrs Noah** | I suppose I'll have to. |
| **Ham** | Father knows what he's doing. |
| **Mrs Noah** | I do hope so! Well, if he's going to have doves, on top of all those other creatures, I'm going to have my potted plants! Someone can fetch my plants for me. *(Japheth returns, carrying the doves. He is followed by the three girls, each carrying a plant)* |
| **Shem** | There, that's the lot. Can't take any more. We're finished. |
| **Ham** | Right! Then let's start loading all this stuff. |
| **Mrs Noah** | Oh, you mustn't do anything without asking your father first! Look, here he comes. *(Mr Noah enters, carrying a hammer. He is holding some string in his mouth)* |

78

| | |
|---|---|
| **Mr Noah** | Ah-wah-wah-wah? Wah-wah-wah-wah. |
| **Girl 1** | What did you say, Mr Noah? |
| **Mr Noah** | Wah-wah. Ah-wah-wah-wah? |
| **Girl 2** | Mr Noah! Your mouth is full of string! |
| **Mrs Noah** | I can never understand what he says – even when his mouth is not full of string! |
| **Girl 3** | Mr Noah – the string! We can't hear what you are saying! |
| **Mr Noah** | (*Taking the string out*) Ah – oh! I said – are you ready? The Ark is finished! |
| **Mrs Noah** | It's finished, is it? Ah, well! Have we really got to go and live in that? |
| **Shem** | I think we ought to start loading, father. |
| **Mr Noah** | Ah – now, let me see. . . Why, yes, of course – no time to lose! Load up, everybody! |
| **Mrs Noah** | Don't take my work-basket, it will only get lost. Here – you had better give it to me to hold, then I shall know where it is. <br> (*Japheth gives it to her*) |
| **Ham** | Come on, then, everyone – give us a hand! Don't forget the small things. <br> (*The sons and their wives start taking some of the furniture from the pile, going off towards the Ark at the side from which Mr Noah entered*) |
| **Mrs Noah** | No time to lose, he says! Why, you've been building this boat, this Ark thing, for months, and now you say there's no time to lose! I don't understand you at all. |
| **Mr Noah** | You will, mother. Just have patience. <br> (*Some neighbours enter. They have stopped on their way to work to have a good laugh at Mr Noah and his family. Some have tools for working in the fields. Some may have shopping baskets. Share these numbered lines among the actors*) |
| **Mr Noah** | Good day to you, neighbours! |
| **Neighbour 1** | 'Morning, admiral! How's the Navy? |
| **Neighbour 2** | All ready for a life on the ocean wave, eh? Finished building your boat, have you, captain? |
| **Mrs Noah** | Oh, it's not a boat! Mr Noah says it's an Ark. |
| **Neighbour 3** | Have it your way. Whatever it is, that thing will never float! |
| **Mr Noah** | You'll see, you'll see. Oh, neighbours, I shall be sorry for you when the flood comes, and the water rises. |
| **Neighbour 4** | It'll need a pretty high tide – that's all I can say. |
| **Neighbour 5** | Seeing as we're miles and miles from the sea! |
| **Mrs Noah** | Oh, you can trust Mr Noah! |
| **Neighbour 6** | Trust him if you like, missus. I prefer dry land. |
| **Neighbour 7** | That's where this boat will stay, too – on dry land. High and dry! |
| **Mr Noah** | One day, I pray – one day – my Ark will be high and dry. God has told me what to do. |
| **Mrs Noah** | But are you sure you understood him, husband? |
| **Neighbour 8** | Never mind all that, Mother Noah. You stay snug in your little house. You stay at home! |
| **Neighbour 9** | Yes, let old Noah go and live in it. You stay! |

| | |
|---|---|
| **Neighbour 9** | Cor! Just listen to that! |
| | *(There is a sound of roaring and screeching)* |
| **Mrs Noah** | Oh, those animals! I don't fancy this at all! |
| **Neighbour 10** | So all you need is patience, eh? Why, you'll just love living in a floating circus – on dry land! |
| **Neighbour 11** | Lovely smell, too – with all those animals! |
| **Mrs Noah** | I do wish I could be sure you know what you're doing. |
| **Mr Noah** | I am acting on the best possible advice, wife. |
| **Neighbour 12** | Listen to him! *(Copying Mr Noah's voice)* I am acting on the best possible advice! Been in touch with the Navy, have you? |
| | *(The sons and their wives return)* |
| **Neighbour 13** | Well blow me down! Here's the crew! |
| **Neighbour 14** | Where are their sailor-suits, Mr Noah? |
| **Ham** | Everything is ready, father. |
| **Shem** | Come on, mother. You must get on board. |
| **Girl 1** | Come along, Mrs Noah. Come and see how we've arranged things. |
| **Girl 2** | You'll soon get used to it. |
| **Girl 3** | Hurry up, Mrs Noah! You'll love it! |
| **Shem** | Give a hand with these last bits and pieces. |
| | *(As they collect the last of the furniture and move off, the neighbours mock them)* |
| **Neighbour 15** | That's right, Mrs Noah. You hang on to your sewing-basket. I reckon you'll have to patch the sails with that! |
| **Neighbour 16** | Or make a shirt for the kangaroo when the weather turns nasty! |
| **Neighbour 17** | He's mad, you know. Old Noah is off his head. |
| **Neighbour 18** | The whole family is mad. |
| **Neighbour 19** | Mad as hatters. Hello! Did I feel rain? |
| **Neighbour 20** | It's only a drop. |
| **Neighbour 21** | We don't get rain at this time of the year. |
| **Neighbour 22** | Well I'm not going to stand here in the wet. Old Noah and his family can get on with it. |
| **Neighbour 23** | Yes, I'm off. *(Calling)* Cheerio, Mr Noah! |
| **Neighbour 24** | Have a good trip! Don't be seasick, now! |
| **Neighbour 25** | *(Shouting)* Bring us back a parrot! |
| **Neighbour 26** | Rain? At this time of the year? That's funny! |
| | *(There is a long roll of distant thunder)* |

First, let us think about the people in the play. You will see, in the list at the beginning, that Mr Noah is the only one whose character is described. What about the sons? And the wives?

But what about Mrs Noah? She might be angry, nagging and sarcastic, because she thinks her husband is being foolish. Or she might be loyal and trusting, perhaps a bit proud of her husband, even though she is worried and confused by everything. The way her part is acted could alter the way others play theirs.

What properties could you use? Can you make the play funnier by the way the actors use some of them?

Then there are the costumes. You might put your actors in the sort of clothes you think they could have worn, using ideas from pictures in books. Or you could dress the actors as if the play were happening today.

# Quiet please, curtain up!

This chapter is about doing a play for an audience of people who have not helped you to put it together.

Decide first who you want to come and watch the play. Your families? Your friends? Perhaps you will decide to show the play to several different audiences.

What kind of story are you going to tell them, and how do you want to perform it? For example, have you made up your mind whether the play should be long or short – or whether to show several short plays? Do you want your audience to laugh a lot? Are they going to enjoy a strange, scary mystery, or a thrilling adventure? Or are you going to tell them about something that has really happened to you or to someone you know about?

Also think very carefully about the play's characters. What kind of people are they? How do they feel about each other, and why? What work do they do? What sort of house, village or town do they live in? If you have a clear idea of things like this, it will help you to believe in the characters, even if you never actually show these facts to the audience during the play.

*Rehearsing is choosing how to do your play and practising it.*

*Work through it, trying out different ways of performing the story and choosing which ones you like best. Think about the characters and how they behave. How old are they? How would they move, talk and wear their clothes? What is your character trying to do and how does he or she feel?*

Having decided to show your play to an audience, you may now want to rehearse it, so that you can get it just as you want it. Rehearsing is choosing how to do the play, and practising it. You have chosen your story and your characters, and now is the time to work through it, trying different ways of performing the story and choosing which ones you like best. Rehearsing also gives everyone a chance to get to know the characters, and to think about the way they behave, how old they are and how they move, talk and wear their clothes.

Rehearsing will give you all a chance to find out how much room you have to act in, and how everyone can move around easily, without getting in each other's way, but letting the audience see everything you want them to. And while you are rehearsing, you can practise speaking very clearly, so that someone sitting in the audience has no difficulty in hearing everything.

So rehearse your play now. And if the way you tell a part of the story seems clear and real, and feels good, try to remember how it feels and get the same feeling next time you do it. If you don't like it, think of a different way of doing it. You want to be sure that each performance you give for your audience tells the story just as clearly as the last one.

82

You can make your play up in any of the ways we've already used in this book. By playing storytelling games, for example. There are also all the ideas for plays at the end of every chapter in this book. You could take any of these and find your own special way of performing them. Or you could take a story you know – a legend or a fairy tale – and make a play out of that.

You may decide that you want to remember your play very exactly, and write down what the characters say. This is called making a play script. There are several ways you could make a script if you want to: you could work your play out very fully, and then write everything down; or you could make your script at the same time as you make the play. For example, you could play some of the storytelling games. When you're pleased with something, write the words and movements down. Then play the game again, this time repeating the bit you have written down, and adding new bits.

If you can borrow a tape recorder, you could make your own script by recording yourselves playing the games, and then choose the best lines spoken by the actors, and write those down. Then everyone could add to them. Next, try acting the script to see if the story is told well. If it isn't, experiment a little more.

*If the way you tell part of the story seems clear, and real, and feels good, try to remember how it feels and get the same feeling next time you do it. If you don't like it, think of a different way of doing it.*

'Why play with plays' may seem a rather strange question to ask now, when you have already spent so much time playing the games in this book! But it is a question that everyone who puts on a play asks themselves at some time or other, and each person has to find their own answer. Plays have been performed for many different reasons. People have wanted to show each other stories about their gods. In China, the fabulous stories of the Monkey King who could make fools out of men were presented with spectacular acrobatic dancing and stage fighting, bright costumes and loud, dramatic music.

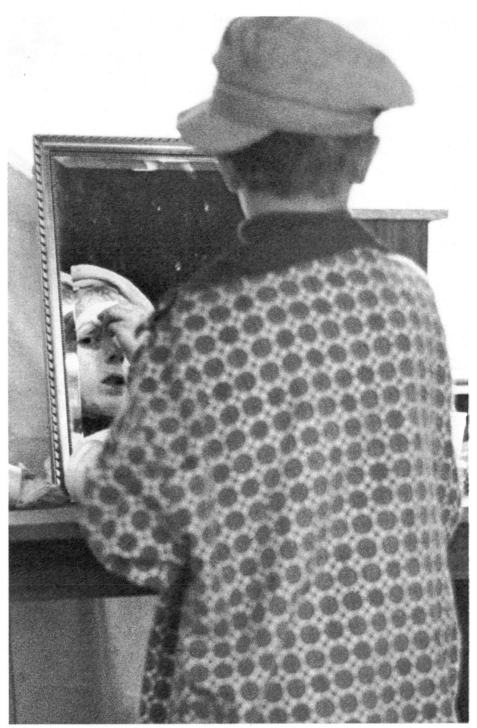

*Now it is time for the final preparations. And this is the time when you have to go right back to the beginning, and remember that you cannot do any of these things without the rest of your group. Your play has been made by a team – you and your friends – and it belongs to all of you.*

In the Middle Ages in Europe, plays performed on carts were stories from the Bible; in India the lives of gods and heroes were danced by exotic Kathakali dancers. Often plays were performed to tell people about some great happening in the country, or to pass on news from other cities and villages. Or there were plays to celebrate the seasons of the year – the end of winter and the excitement of spring sowing and planting; the end of summer and the rich harvests of autumn. People have also wanted to mark some great event in their lives by plays – the birth of a baby, a marriage, or the tragedy of a death.

Playwrights and actors became interested in showing how wars have started, and in stories about people who are hungry for power. And they have also shown stories about the lives of ordinary people, about the kinds of problems they have to solve, the adventures they have, or just what happens when they fall in love.

In the modern theatre we have all sorts of different plays to choose from. Some are just for fun – so that the audience can go out to laugh and enjoy themselves. Others include a lot of singing and dancing. Sometimes a play can be a way of making people think about things which may never happen to them, but which they see happening to other people in the play. That way they can learn a little more about them.

In some countries troupes of actors go into schools, factories and other work places, or act in the streets of towns. They perform plays about problems which they think are important and which they want people to think about – safety at work, or whether to build a new motorway or park, or how the factory should be run.

And now you should think again about why you want to do your play. It is up to you. It is your play, to share with an audience you have chosen.

It is time for the final preparations. Your story is made up, and you have rehearsed it. You have thought about your characters and their dialogue, and you know how you want to act them. You have experimented with costumes and masks, if you want them, and they are all ready for the actors to put on.

Your sound effects, or any other special effects, have been practised and are ready to be used. Each of you has chosen the job you want to do during the performance – who is going to help people with their costumes, who is going to put up any scenery, arrange furniture and get the props ready at the side of the stage, so that the actors know where to find them.

If there is a stage fight in the play, you have rehearsed it very thoroughly so that it is safe, and no one could possibly get hurt, but it looks most dramatic and dangerous!

This is the moment when you have to go right back to the beginning, and remember that you cannot do any of these things without the rest of your group. Your play has been made by a team – you and your friends, and it belongs to all of you. Now, when you are about to share it with an outside audience for the first time, you must remember to help each other, so that each of you can do your very best to make the performance enjoyable for both you and your audience.

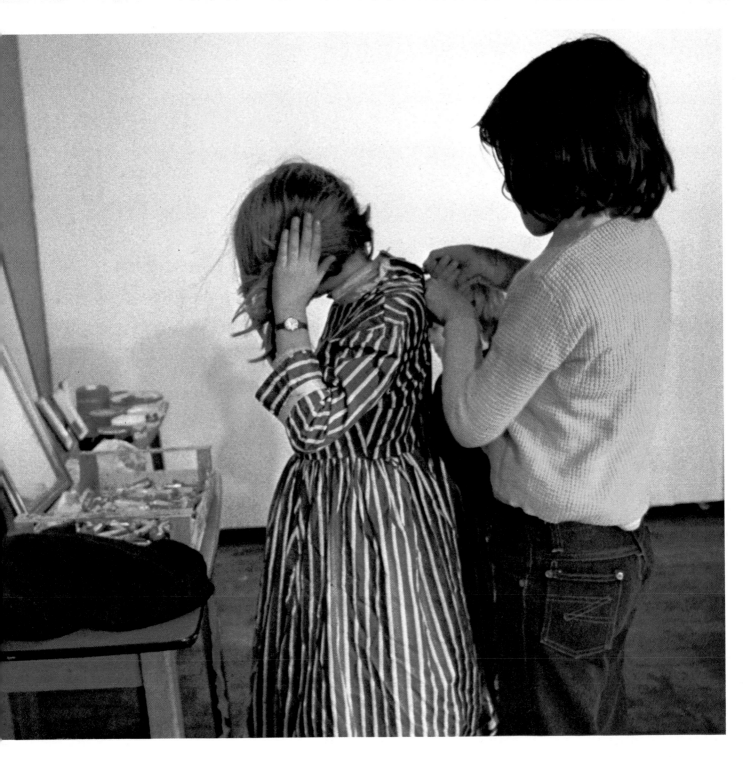

*When you are about to share your play with an outside audience for the first time, you must remember to help each other, so that each of you can do your very best to make the performance enjoyable for both you and your audience.*

It is time to go back to the very first games with which we started our book – the games we used to warm ourselves up and get to know each other. Play them now. Stretch and explore the space around you, so that every part of your body is woken up. Play the mirror game, with different people. Here is a good game for warming up and getting your thoughts moving. Think of something very interesting to tell a partner. Both of you must tell each other your own story at the same time and make it so interesting that you force your partner to stop talking and start listening to you instead. But make sure you play this game where the audience can't hear!

Your audience is arriving! Welcome them to the play. They know nothing about it. You are sharing something with them which has been your secret, and they are probably just as excited as you are.

Perhaps you have written out a programme, telling them the name of the play, the characters in it, who the actors are, and the names of everyone else who has worked on the play or helped you put it together. And don't forget people who have helped you in other ways, loaned you something to use, for example – costumes or furniture, or even the room itself. Now is the time to give the programme out so that the audience can read it.

*Perhaps you have written out a programme telling them the name of the play, the characters and actors and everyone who has helped to put the play on.*

*Give it out to the audience as they arrive, so that they can read it as they wait for the play to begin.*

Every audience is made up of different people, and different audiences can make your play feel quite different. They may laugh much more than you thought they would, for example. If they do laugh at a funny bit, leave them time to laugh before you say the next line, otherwise they won't hear it. Or they may sit in hushed quiet throughout, listening to every word you say! And you will all feel their mood during the performance.

The play is about to begin. The audience is seated. They are waiting eagerly for you to start. The noise of their conversation dies away. All is silent.

It's over to you now! Good luck!

Every audience is made up of
different people, and different
audiences can make your play
feel quite different. They may
laugh much more than you
thought they would. They may
give loud gasps when something
surprises or shocks them. Or they
may sit very quietly, listening
carefully to everything your
actors say, so that they don't
miss anything.

Whatever happens, your play
will have been a new event for
them – something to enjoy and
think about afterwards.

# A play for you to finish

The first part of this play is written out for you here, with the words the characters speak and some of the actions. But the ending is a mystery. It is up to you to finish the play in whatever way you want to.

The play takes place in a room in a deserted house. A teacher and her pupils are on a school outing.

The characters are: **a teacher** – this can be a man or woman (the script is written as though it is a woman, but you can easily change the word 'miss' to 'sir', if you decide you'd rather give this part to a boy).

**The children** – you can have as few or as many as you like. They don't all have to speak. Once you have decided how many 'children' to have in the play, read their parts carefully and decide which 'child' will say what. Then number the 'children' – Child 1, Child 2 and so on, or give them names. Write these numbers or names on the script beside the words you want each character to say.

What actions do you think the characters will make while they speak? Who are they talking to? What can you tell about the characters from their words? How are you going to suggest or show the rainstorm and the deserted house to your audience?

**The deserted house:** a mystery

*The play starts with the teacher walking on to the stage*

| | |
|---|---|
| **Teacher** | *(Calling)* This will do! Come on, everybody! Quickly! *(The children run on. Two of them are carrying a basket with a picnic in it)* |
| **Child** | Oh, miss, it's started to rain. |
| **Child** | Is there going to be a storm, miss? |
| **Teacher** | Hurry up – everybody inside! Shut the door. |
| **Child** | Listen to the wind! |
| **Child** | Are you wet? I am. |
| **Child** | A bit. Not much. |
| **Teacher** | There! Now we'll be all right. Is everybody here? |
| **Child** | Is there going to be a storm, miss? |
| **Teacher** | It looks very black, doesn't it? I think there will be. |
| **Child** | I heard it thunder as we ran through the garden. |
| **Child** | Listen! It's raining really hard now. |
| **Child** | Where are we, miss? |
| **Teacher** | I don't know. Some old, deserted house. It's lucky we found it. |
| **Child** | Good thing it wasn't locked up. |
| **Child** | *(Finding some large boxes in the corner of the room)* Look what I've found. |
| **Teacher** | Good! Bring those boxes here. We can sit on them. *(They settle down, some on the floor, some on the boxes, and some looking out of the window)* |
| **Teacher** | Well, we can't carry on with our outing now. |
| **Child** | What'll we do, miss? Can we play a game? *(There is a loud crack of thunder and a big gust of wind)* |
| **Children** | Ooh! Did you hear that! Isn't it loud! |
| **Child** | I don't like thunder. |
| **Child** | *(At the window)* Thunder isn't dangerous. It can't hurt you. |

| | |
|---|---|
| **Child** | Lightning is dangerous. That can hurt you. You ought to come away from the window. |
| **Teacher** | We'll be safe enough here until the storm stops. |
| **Child** | Whose house is this? |
| **Teacher** | I don't know. It's empty, anyway. It doesn't look as though anyone's lived here for a long, long time. |
| **Child** | It sounds all hollow. |
| **Child** | Yes. Listen what happens when I jump. |
| **Child** | That's because it's empty. There's no furniture or carpets. |
| **Child** | But we've got the boxes to sit on. |
| **Child** | It's very dirty. |
| **Child** | It looks as if it's been empty for ever and ever! |
| **Child** | It's scarey! Really creepy! |
| **Child** | And gloomy. |
| **Child** | And cold. |
| **Child** | Oh, miss – do you think it's haunted? |
| **Teacher** | Haunted? Don't be silly! Now, what about this game? Let's play something to pass the time. <br> *(There is a huge, long crash of thunder. They fall silent as the wind roars again and then dies down)* |
| **Child** | I don't like it here! |
| **Child** | Nor do I! |
| **Child** | I *hate* thunder! |
| **Child** | Perhaps this *is* a haunted house! |
| **Child** | Oh, miss. Tell us a story – tell us a ghost story! |
| **Child** | Go on, miss. Tell us a story about a haunted house. |
| **Child** | Like this one. |
| **Child** | It's gone dark! Why's it gone dark? |
| **Teacher** | It's those black thunder clouds. |
| **Child** | It always goes dark in a storm. <br> *(There is another thunder crash, and more wind)* |
| **Child** | Bang! Crash-bang-crash! |
| **Teacher** | Sit down quietly! It'll be over soon and then we can leave. <br> *(There is a rumble of thunder. During the next few lines the wind dies into the background)* |
| **Teacher** | There! That thunder was much farther away. |
| **Child** | It's still raining, though. You can hear it. |
| **Child** | Come on, miss – tell us a ghost story! |
| **Children** | Yes, miss, please! |
| **Teacher** | All right. But first, why don't we eat our lunch here? |
| **Children** | I'm starving! What's there to eat, miss? <br> *(They unpack their basket)* |
| **Teacher** | You two, hand things round, and then, while you're eating, I can tell you a story. |
| **Child** | A ghost story, miss. About a haunted house. |
| **Teacher** | Settle down. I'll think of something. <br> *(The children hand round food and drink)* |
| **Child** | Come on, miss. Once upon a time there was a haunted house. |
| **Teacher** | *(Starting the story, helped by some of the children)* <br> Yes, once upon a time there was a haunted house. . . |
| **Child** | And some children had to shelter there. . . |
| **Child** | From a terrible storm. . . |
| **Child** | And the lightning flashed and the thunder rolled. . . |

| | |
|---|---|
| **Teacher** | But no one was frightened. They were far too sensible. And, of course, they did not know that the house was haunted. . . |
| **Child** | But, suddenly, there was a terrible noise. . . |
| | *(Just at that moment there* IS *a terrible noise! There is a tremendous rattling crash, like a big piece of furniture falling over. They all stop and listen)* |
| **Teacher** | Whatever was that? |
| **Child** | It was up there! Upstairs! |
| | *(They huddle together and look up)* |
| **Child** | It sounded like something being knocked over. |
| **Child** | Or like a big picture falling down! |
| **Children** | Ooh! |
| **Child** | Ssh! Listen! |
| | *(They are quiet. There is a squeak, and a creaking)* |
| **Child** | Ooh, miss! I'm frightened! |
| **Teacher** | It's only the wind. Nothing to be frightened of. Nothing at all. Eat up your food. |
| | *(There is a bang)* |
| **Child** | A door! Upstairs! |
| **Child** | Upstairs! Someone banged a door! |
| **Child** | Oh, miss – there's someone upstairs! |
| **Teacher** | Nonsense! The house is empty. It was the wind. |
| | *(They listen to the wind. Then there is a loud, long drawn-out creak. Two children scream)* |
| **Teacher** | Stop that nonsense at once! You're making yourselves frightened. Stay where you are. I'll look. |
| | *(Two big thumps are heard)* |
| **Children** | Don't go, miss! Don't go! Stay here! Stay with us! |
| | *(There are two more thumps)* |
| **Child** | Footsteps! |
| **Teacher** | Rubbish! |
| **Child** | It was! It was! |
| | *(Two more thumps – louder)* |
| **Child** | It's on the stairs! |
| **Child** | Something is coming down the stairs! |
| | *(Two louder thumps)* |
| **Child** | Help! Help! |
| **Teacher** | Be quiet! |
| | *(The noise is now just outside the room, coming closer)* |
| **Children** | Ooh! *(They back away from the door)* |
| **Teacher** | *(Calling)* Who is it? Who's there? |
| | *(Something thumps the door)* |
| **Child** | *(In a loud whisper)* The door! Look at the door! It's opening! |
| | *(Slowly the door begins to open)* |

Now what happens? Who (or what) is coming through the door?

# Index

## List of plays

## Acknowledgements

Editor
**Beverley Birch**

Designer
**Martin Stringer**

Artists
**Peter Dennis**    14-16, 30-32, 46-48, 62-64, 78-80, 92-94
**Maggie Read**    36, 37, 40, 41, 56-61, 66-76, 89

Picture research
**Leonora Elford**

Production
**Philip Hughes**

Teacher panel
**Steve Allen**
**Penny Anderson**
**David Montgomerie**
**Dawn Sanders**
**David Urie**
**Janet Young**

Unicorn workshop leaders
**Gail Haley**
**Geoff Larder**
**Brenda Kempner**
**John Bowler**

Plays by
**Richard Blythe**    14-16, 30-32, 46-48, 62-64, 78-80, 92-94

The publishers would like to thank the children and staff of
Hackney Free and Parochial Junior School and Keyworth
Primary School for their help in the production of this book.

Author's acknowledgements:
**Nicholas Barter** would like to thank: Penny who typed and
made valuable suggestions; Dominic and Lucy who taught him
about children; all those actors and directors from whom he
learned and borrowed and with whom he has developed these
games, especially Keith Johnstone and Viola Spolin.

Printed in Italy